T0317804

AT
NONNA'S
TABLE

AT
NONNA'S
TABLE

One Italian family's recipes, shared with love

Paola Bacchia

Smith
Street
Books

Grazie per tutto mamma, sarai sempre nel mio cuore,
dalla tua Paoletta xxx

Livia Ida Carli, Monfalcone (1947).

CONTENTS

Introduction   9

Chapters

SOUPS & SMALLER DISHES   15
PASTA & RICE   47
MOSTLY VEGETABLES   67
FISH & MEAT   115
SWEET THINGS   149

Stories

From Mansuè to Melbourne   20
Pra dei Gai   38
Memories of Nonna's table   54
Factory days: ham & cheese
    toasties for lunch   94
Menu planning   124
Mamma & her cookbooks   140
An Instagram nonna   164
Stories of fruit & jam   196

Thank you   206
About the author   208
Index   210

Plumrae, Box Hill South, Melbourne (1951).

Introduction

My mother, Livia, loved telling stories. Having just finished a delicious meal at her kitchen table, over empty plates and creased floral napkins, we would listen as she told us about her aunt Rica, who would stretch the dough for *crostoli* over the *fogolar* (hearth) with her hands, or how she would go with her uncle to the Pra dei Gai (a field in her home town of Mansuè) when the sun was setting, and he would catch fish for their dinner from the shallow stream using his bare hands. Her stories were joyful and vivid, and the family table was just the place for sharing them, when our bellies were happy from the food she had made and our hearts were full.

Livia arrived in Australia in 1950 as a young bride, into what was a food culture void. Her first experience of this was at the Bonegilla migrant camp, where she and my father spent the first month of their life together in Australia. The stories of those miserable weeks and the mess hall continued to be told well into the 2000s. 'You won't believe what they fed us,' my father would say. 'Boiled mutton and cabbage!' We would feign horror and surprise, but knew the stories well.

Mamma had not always cooked. She had worked front of house in the family bar/tavern, but never in the kitchen. The simple meals the family ate were prepared by her mother or one of the hired cooks. Once married, she quickly discovered that her new husband's mood was driven almost entirely by the state of his stomach – so she set herself the task of learning to cook. At the start, there was no one to teach her, and no cookbooks in Italian from which to learn. Mamma would recount the story of their first New Year's Eve in Australia, when they had invited friends over and spinach risotto was on the menu. She failed to properly wash the soil from the spinach leaves, throwing it into the pot only lightly rinsed. When dinner was served, the guests politely picked at the gritty rice dish – and my father never let her forget it! She asked her brother Fidenzio, who was migrating to Australia in 1952, to bring a cookbook in Italian, and started attending an Italian social club, where she could get tips from other ladies from Italy's north-east. Within a short while, she learnt to make meals that drew praise even from my rather exacting father. Over time, her repertoire and reputation among their friends grew.

The children came along, then the grandchildren. After a full week of work in the factory, Saturdays were for cleaning the house, and Sundays were for having the family over for lunch. Meals were simple but delicious – a traditional three-course Sunday menu of pasta, meat and vegetables, followed by dessert and coffee. There was much work to be done to prepare the meal on a Sunday morning, but Mamma didn't want any help in the kitchen. My assigned task was to set the table in the dining room. How she managed

> "
> **The family table was just the place for sharing her stories, when our bellies were happy and our hearts were full.**

multiple pots and trays to feed the seven of us – which included the two older grandchildren at the time – every week after working in the factory and cleaning the house, I will never know.

She and my father retired at the same time and they suddenly had a lot more free time. My father had always been interested in eating food, though never in cooking it – bar one memorable and often recounted occasion when my mother was unwell and bedridden. He made a batch of meat ragù from scratch, disturbing her rest with non-stop questions on the method, and he managed to eat almost the whole pot while tasting it. He took great interest in watching cooking shows on TV. He would scribble down the ingredients and method, then hand my mother a piece of paper with his handwritten notes. So, she began to try new and more elaborate dishes and cooking methods – and when they started going to an Italian social club that had members from southern Italy, this added a whole new dimension to her cooking. She started using ingredients such as dried olives, capers and chilli flakes in her recipes. She would stuff cuttlefish, poach veal for *vitello tonnato,* blister tomatoes for spicy puttanesca. She learnt to debone a whole chicken in 12 minutes. With a couple of fairly swift moves, the entire carcass would emerge in one piece, so that she could stuff the body, sew it up and then, once roasted, the chicken could be sliced whole, a ring of tender white meat encircling a filling of minced veal and pork studded with pistachios and stripes of pressed ham.

My father had a fondness for sweets, and there was always something homemade and sweet in the pantry for when friends dropped by. In addition to our traditional Italian desserts, the *Australian Women's Weekly Cakes and Slices Cookbook*

became a favourite, and oats, coconut and brown sugar made their way into her repertoire. She loved hosting and was generous to a fault with the food she made. For years my daughter, Tamara, and I would go there for lunch on a Sunday and would come home with a basket full of goodies: freshly picked leafy green radicchio, lemons and zucchini (courgettes) from my father's backyard, a tray of lasagne, a jar of basil pesto and half a ricotta cake, all fresh from Mamma's kitchen.

When my father passed away, my mother was in her mid-80s and suddenly found she did not have to answer to anyone and could cook exactly as she pleased. She missed him terribly, but was also somewhat relieved that at times she could have leftovers for lunch, or vegetable soup for dinner, without hearing any grumbles. Over time, Mamma's cooking repertoire became smaller. When there is only one person eating, it doesn't seem worth making cannelloni, or an elaborate cake. And as Mamma neared 90, her health declined and she wasn't as interested in cooking anything apart from her staples: hearty vegetable soup, meat ragù (which we called

---

"

There was always something homemade and sweet in the pantry.

---

sugo) and a seeming endless repertoire of braised dishes involving vegetables, the leftovers of which she turned into risotto when we went over for lunch.

She spent over two years in aged care. She had a room surrounded by familiar furniture, framed photos of family and her favourite quilt on the bed. But she found the change of routine difficult; she had stopped feeling useful. She missed donning an apron and making lunches using her well-worn chopping board and less-than-sharp knives. She missed collecting herbs from the garden, watering the plants on the terrace, having the children and grandchildren over for lunch and, at night in bed, hearing the familiar noises and creaks of the house she had lived in for over 40 years. She passed away suddenly one night in mid-2020, aged 92. I miss her every day.

This book is a collection of dishes that Mamma made – our family recipes, and of those inspired by her, recalling lunches she made for the extended family, for celebrations with friends or just for us two. It includes stories of her life that highlight her connection to her family, her community and to her table. She is my inspiration in so many ways.

Her unconditional love for us and her memories inspired the food she gave us over the long decades of her life, and this is at the heart of her recipes. I hope the recipes that you now have in your hands give you joy, and may you share them with love.

> "
> **This book is a collection of dishes that Mamma made – our family recipes, and of those inspired by her, recalling lunches she made for the extended family, for celebrations with friends or just for us two.**

Piazza Grande, Oderzo, Veneto (2022).

SOUPS & SMALLER DISHES

1. Figs with prosciutto & blue cheese
2. Asparagus gratin with walnuts
3. Leek prosciutto bundles
4. Pickled vegetables
5. Grilled vegetable platter
6. Zucchini & potato soup with sage
7. Spinach & polenta soup
8. Chicken egg-drop soup
9. Everyday vegetable soup with basil pesto
10. Sausage & spinach frittata
11. Focaccia with milk

Figs were Mamma's favourite fruit. She had a knack of knowing exactly which one was perfect to eat, and which one was not yet ripe or past its best. She would give the fig a firm squeeze and if it easily yielded and bounced back lightly, then it was good. For this recipe, the figs do not need to be absolutely perfectly ripe; even a slightly dry one will work. The sweetness of the figs is deliciously balanced by the saltiness of the prosciutto, the creaminess of the cheese and the mild acidity of the balsamic glaze.

Figs with prosciutto & blue cheese

FICHI, PROSCIUTTO E GORGONZOLA

SERVES 6

6 large figs (or 12 small ones)
60 g (2 oz) creamy blue cheese,
    such as Gorgonzola
      Dolce Latte
6 large thin slices prosciutto
balsamic glaze, for drizzling

Preheat the oven to 170°C (340°F) fan-forced. Line a baking tray with baking paper.

Cut the figs in half, from the stem towards the base, but don't slice all the way through. You want the figs to still be connected at the base. Place a small amount of blue cheese inside each fig, dividing it equally. Close the figs up and wrap a prosciutto slice around each fig, to hold them together.

Place the figs upright on the baking tray, spacing them apart. Roast for 6–10 minutes, depending on the size of the figs, until the prosciutto is partially crisp, the cheese melted and the figs warmed through.

Serve warm, with a drizzle of balsamic glaze.

In the 1970s, 'flexi time' was a new thing. The paint factory where Papà worked allowed him to work extra hours from Monday through to Thursday, then finish work early on a Friday. That's when he would do the weekly shopping for the family, broadly following Mamma's handwritten shopping list – leaving out some of the items he didn't like, much to her chagrin, but buying extra of whatever produce was in season. Finding asparagus heralded the start of spring, he would happily buy plenty, so Mamma could make asparagus risotto, asparagus with eggs, asparagus bundles with prosciutto, or asparagus gratin.

Mamma would use dried breadcrumbs in her gratin, but I love using crushed walnuts, making the dish gluten free and accenting the asparagus wonderfully.

Asparagus gratin with walnuts

ASPARAGI GRATINATI

SERVES 4

750 g (1 lb 11 oz) asparagus spears; thicker stems are better
40 ml (1¼ fl oz) dry white wine (or reserved asparagus cooking water)
40 g (1½ oz) unsalted butter
50 g (½ cup) shelled walnuts, coarsely crushed
75 g (¾ cup) grated parmesan
handful of chopped parsley, to serve
juice of ½ lemon

Preheat the oven to 180°C (350°F) fan-forced.

Trim the whiter woody base off the asparagus spears, but not too much. (The centre of the trimmed woody tip is usually quite tender, so if you'd like to keep these, you can simply peel away the tougher outer skin using a vegetable peeler.)

Bring a large saucepan of salted water to the boil and carefully drop in the asparagus spears. Cook for 2–5 minutes, depending on their thickness, so they are partially cooked, but still have a bit of bite. Drain and pat dry. Reserve 40 ml (1¼ fl oz) of the cooking water, if not using wine.

Smear a tablespoon of the butter across the base of a shallow ovenproof serving dish that will fit all the asparagus snugly in a single layer. Arrange the asparagus in the dish. Drizzle with the wine (or reserved cooking water). Scatter on the crushed walnuts, parmesan and a few grinds of black pepper, then dot with the remaining butter.

Bake on the top shelf of your oven for 10–12 minutes, until the cheese has melted and is golden. Serve warm, scattered with the parsley and sprinkled with the lemon juice.

FROM MANSUÈ TO MELBOURNE

Livia Ida Carli was born in 1927 in the small agricultural town of Mansuè in north-eastern Italy, to Francesco and Carolina. She was the youngest of five children, and shared her bed with her two sisters, Livia taking the middle spot. They lived in a pretty Swiss chalet–inspired house designed by her uncle Vincenzo, who was killed during World War I. Her father, a builder by trade, finished the house in time for all five children to be born there, the first in 1921. The family ran bars and taverns and in 1937 moved to the town of Monfalcone to expand their business.

Livia started working in one of her parents' taverns, in the heart of town. She was a beautiful young woman and had many admirers. She saved up money to have her picture taken by a local photographer, and it hung in the window of the photographic studio. One of these admirers was my father, Nello, a war refugee from Istria. He met her at the bar where she worked and wooed her for six months. They married in 1948.

My father had been a soldier during the war, and the land in which he was born had been ceded to communist Yugoslavia in 1947. He moved to Monfalcone with his family and had a burning desire to find a new place to call home. My mother was somewhat reluctant, but agreed to spend time in Paris, where she had an aunt, to see if that was where their future lay. It didn't work out, so my father started exploring further afield and decided on America – but, faced with a lengthy waiting time for a passage there, they opted for Australia instead. In early April 1950, after months spent in migrant camps criss-crossing Italy – Rome, Barletta and, finally, Bagnoli – Nello and Livia boarded the General Greely, bound for Melbourne. My grandparents decided to surprise their youngest daughter and made the trek by train from Monfalcone to Bagnoli, near Naples. As fate would have it, my grandparents did not receive the letter from my mother telling them when the ship was departing. They arrived the day after my parents had sailed.

Livia and Nello landed at Melbourne's Station Pier on 13 May 1950, and within a day were whisked by train to a former army camp in country Victoria called Bonegilla. The camp was overflowing with residents, some 7000 at the time. Countless stories have been told about the food at Bonegilla – horror tales of boiled mutton, soggy vegetables and cardboard-like bread. It comes as no surprise that, in 1952, the migrants revolted against the food in an incident called The Spaghetti Riots, where angry Italians apparently emptied plates of spaghetti (presumably the tinned variety) on the door of the camp director's house in protest. There was an obvious solution to the problem of food: ask the European residents to be the cooks, which is what eventually transpired.

My mother cried every day for the first six months. She missed her family terribly. She could not speak the new language or understand the strange culture. The first time she and my father went to a pub for a drink, in the town of Albury near Bonegilla, she was shooed into what was called the Ladies Lounge, as no women were allowed at the bar! The food culture was foreign to her; food was fried in dripping, and olive oil was only available from a pharmacy. Beer was the preferred beverage, and the Australians would tease the Italians for drinking wine, which they called 'plonk'.

Within a year of arriving, my father went to the Department of Immigration and in broken English stated that he wanted to return to Italy. They had migrated as part of an assisted passage scheme for Europeans upended by the war, which required them to work in Australia for two years in exchange for the journey. He was told by a gruff official that to do this he would need to pay back the cost of the ship passage and compensate the government for cutting the contract short – or wait until the two years had passed, and then leave. Either way, it was a financial impossibility with their factory wages.

So they worked hard and saved as much as they could. And over time, they grew used to their new life. They purchased a block of land in what was then a sparsely populated Melbourne suburb, Box Hill South. With the help of my mother's brother Fidenzio, who arrived in 1952, my father built our first home. Then came another brother, Livio, and his wife Dina – and by 1954 the siblings were living in houses on adjoining blocks, creating their own close-knit community. Mamma had become quite the cook by then, and as they were one of the few families with a large house, they frequently hosted parties where, helped by my aunt Dina, she would cook spreads of food that tasted just like home.

These delicious bundles are a favourite at home. Although asparagus is more commonly used in this dish, their season is so short, whereas leeks are around from autumn through to spring, making this version a welcome and more regular addition to the dining table. I calculate one medium-sized leek per person, though I urge you to make a few extra – they won't go to waste! If the leeks are thin, you might like to place more than one in a bundle. This dish is based on a recipe in one of the classic Lisa Biondi cookbooks (see page 141).

Leek prosciutto bundles

MAZZETTI DI PORRI AL FORNO

SERVES 4

5–6 leeks
25 g (1 oz) butter
5–6 slices prosciutto
40 g (1½ oz) shaved parmesan

To prepare the leeks, remove the tougher outer layers, then trim the green tops and the roots from the white ends. Wash in plenty of water to remove any soil hiding in the looser layers.

Bring a large wide saucepan of salted water to the boil. Carefully drop in the leeks. Cook for 6–10 minutes, until the leeks are just tender when tested with a fork; you don't want them to be too soft and falling apart. Remove the leeks with tongs and give them a good shake to remove the excess water. Lay them on a clean tea towel to continue draining, then pat them dry.

Preheat the oven to 170°C (340°F) fan-forced.

Select a baking dish that will allow the leeks to lay flat and not overlap each other. Smear the base with a bit of the butter. Wrap each leek in a slice of prosciutto on the diagonal. Place in your dish, side by side.

Melt the remaining butter and pour over the leeks. Top with the parmesan and a few grinds of black pepper. Bake for 10–12 minutes, spooning on some of the butter in the base of the pan halfway through.

Serve warm, with crusty bread to mop up the sauce.

My parents held Christmas Eve parties in the late 1970s through to the 1980s, where my mother would host up to 12 people for an Italian-style smorgasbord. Photos from the time show people laughing, clearly having a terrific time, with a drink in one hand and a cigarette in the other. In the background you can see the lounge room wall, covered in red-brick patterned wallpaper, the teak lounge setting with plump brown and beige striped cushioning on the shag pile carpet. Guests would be welcomed with platters of cured meats, cubes of cheese ... and pickled vegetables, or *giardiniera*.

This recipe is from my dear friend Verdiana. The list of vegetables in the recipe below is not exhaustive; you could also include others such as cabbage, celery and onion.

Pickled vegetables
GIARDINIERA

MAKES 2 × 700 ML (23½ FL OZ) JARS

1 small carrot
¼ small fennel bulb
1 small bell pepper (capsicum)
¼ small cauliflower
3–4 broccolini stalks
1 small zucchini (courgette)
1 short cucumber
1.5 litres (6 cups) white wine vinegar
200 ml (7 fl oz) white wine
25 g (1 oz) sugar
22 g (¾ oz) salt
8–10 whole peppercorns
2 fresh bay leaves
2 garlic cloves, peeled and sliced (optional – see Note)
extra virgin olive oil, for covering the pickles

Wash two 700 ml (23½ fl oz) glass jars, and their lids, in hot soapy water and rinse well. Place the upturned jars and lids in an 80°C (175°F) fan-forced oven to dry for 20 minutes. Turn the oven off and leave them there until ready to use.

Prepare all your vegetables before you start, keeping them separated as they will have different cooking times. Wash, peel and chop individual vegetables as required, then cut into batons of roughly the same size.

Pour the vinegar and wine into a saucepan large enough to fit all the ingredients. Add 750 ml (3 cups) of water. Slowly bring to the boil, then add the sugar and salt, stirring well until dissolved. Keep on a simmer and have a timer ready.

Add the carrot, then start the timer. After 1 minute, add the fennel. After another 1 minute, add the bell pepper. Continue adding the cauliflower, broccolini, zucchini and cucumber at 1-minute intervals. After the cucumber has cooked for 1 minute, drain the vegetables, discarding the brine. Lay the vegetables out on a clean tea towel. Leave to cool.

Place half the vegetables in each jar using tongs. Add a few peppercorns and a bay leaf to each jar, and the garlic, if using. Pack the vegetable batons in tightly, leaving a space of about 5 mm (¼ in) at the top of each jar. Cover the vegetables with olive oil and seal the jars.

Store the jars in the fridge. The pickles will be ready after 1–2 days and will keep for 3–4 months. They are wonderful on antipasto platters.

NOTE: I only add the garlic if I'm intending to use the pickles within a month, as the garlic does not keep well.

Top left: Eating spaghetti with friends, Bonegilla, Australia (1950).
Opposite: Livia's home in via Fossabiuba, Mansuè, Veneto (1990).
This page: Plumrae, Box Hill South, Melbourne (1951).

Summer brings a wealth of vegetables to the table, and at our house this was mostly via my father's garden. As much as he disliked the way they took over the garden, he planted zucchini religiously every year. In later years there were also eggplants and bell peppers. When the weather was really hot, Mamma would make platters of grilled garden-fresh vegetables infused with garlic and olive oil, plus a good shake of salt. This was often accompanied by a frittata, grilled fish or meat, or even just bread and wedges of hard cheese. Simple but so delicious. When serving, I also add a drizzle of good-quality balsamic vinegar for a lovely acidic/sweet balance, and sometimes a sprinkling of herbs, such as dried oregano or fresh parsley.

Grilled vegetable platter

VERDURE ALLA GRIGLIA

SERVES 4

1 garlic clove, thinly sliced
80–100 ml (2½–3½ fl oz) extra
    virgin olive oil
1 red bell pepper (capsicum)
1 large eggplant (aubergine)
1 large zucchini (courgette)
8 asparagus spears
chopped parsley, for sprinkling
balsamic vinegar, for drizzling

Preheat the oven to 180°C (350°F) fan-forced. Place the garlic in a jar with the olive oil to infuse.

Place the bell pepper on a baking tray and roast for about 25 minutes, turning over as needed, until the skin is blistered and charred. Place in a bowl, cover with an upturned plate and leave to sweat for a few minutes. Remove the charred skin, stem and seeds, then cut the flesh into thick strips.

Cut the eggplant and zucchini into 4–6 mm (¼ inch) slices, using a mandoline or sharp knife. Trim the woody ends of the asparagus spears.

Place a cast-iron grill pan on the stovetop over medium–high heat. (Alternatively, you could heat a barbecue grill plate to medium–high.)

Working in batches, brush the vegetables on one side with the garlicky olive oil and place that side down on the grill. After a few minutes, brush the other side with olive oil, before turning over with tongs.

Arrange all the grilled vegetables on a serving platter. Serve scattered with salt and parsley and a drizzle of balsamic vinegar.

If not serving immediately, store the vegetables in a covered container, and only drizzle with vinegar just before serving.

Mamma would often make simple soups focusing on one main seasonal vegetable. A rule of thumb was whatever the weight of that vegetable, there would be an equal amount of potato in the soup. This is her version of zucchini soup, perfect for using up the summer glut from the vegetable garden – either your own, if you are lucky enough to have one, or a friendly neighbour's. Sage is a lovely addition to this soup.

Zucchini & potato soup with sage

ZUPPA DI ZUCCHINI E PATATE CON SALVIA

SERVES 6

30 g (1 oz) butter
1 tablespoon extra virgin
    olive oil
1 large white or brown onion,
    roughly chopped
750 g (1 lb 11 oz) zucchini
    (courgettes), cut into 3 cm
    (1¼ inch) rounds
750 g (1 lb 11 oz) all-purpose
    potatoes, peeled and cut
    into 6–8 pieces each
1.25 litres (5 cups) warm
    chicken stock (see page 34),
    or 1.25 litres (5 cups) boiling
    water plus a good-quality
    stock (bouillon) cube
4–5 sage leaves

Warm the butter and olive oil in a large heavy-based saucepan over low heat. Add the onion and sprinkle with a good pinch of salt. After about 7 minutes, when the onion softens and becomes translucent, add the zucchini and potato, stirring well until warmed through.

Pour in the stock (or boiling water and stock cube) and add the sage leaves. Once the stock starts bubbling away, cover the pan, reduce the heat and leave to simmer for 1 hour. By now the potatoes and zucchini should be falling apart.

Remove from the heat and allow to cool a little, before processing the soup into a green-flecked cream using a hand-cranked mouli, stick blender or a food processor.

Once smooth, return the soup to the pan and warm through. Season with salt and freshly cracked black pepper to taste, and your soup is ready.

The recipe for spinach and polenta soup is from Friuli-Venezia Giulia, the region in north-east Italy where Mamma's family moved after they left the Veneto. It is simple but surprisingly hearty. The dish can be enhanced by crumbling in a couple of pork sausages – or even some finely chopped pancetta – at the start, and/or replacing the vegetable stock with a homemade meat stock. The addition of parmesan is not traditional, but adds a lovely creamy and salty edge, and is my preferred way to enjoy this thick, rustic soup.

Spinach & polenta soup

PAPAROT

SERVES 6-8

2 large bunches of English spinach, about 800 g (1 lb 12 oz) in total
40 g (1½ oz) butter
2 tablespoons extra virgin olive oil
1 garlic clove, crushed or finely chopped
1.6 litres (54 fl oz) warm homemade vegetable stock or 1.6 litres (54 fl oz) boiling water plus a good-quality stock (bouillon) cube
120 g (4½ oz) coarse polenta (not instant)
2–3 handfuls of grated parmesan

Wash the spinach several times in plenty of water until it drains clean. Remove the roots and any damaged leaves. Place a large saucepan over medium–high heat. Add the spinach, in batches if needed, and allow to wilt, using tongs to help push the leaves down. Once wilted, remove from the heat. Drain the spinach, reserving all the liquid that drains from the pan for your stock. Chop the leaves and set aside.

Warm the butter and olive oil in a large heavy-based saucepan over medium–low heat. When the butter has melted, add the garlic and cook for a few minutes, until fragrant. (If using sausages or pancetta, add it here and allow to start to colour slightly.)

Stir in the drained spinach, coating it with the butter and oil. Pour in the stock and season with salt to taste. Slowly allow the mixture to come to the boil. Shower in the polenta, stirring well with a large wooden spoon so the polenta doesn't form lumps. The mixture should simmer slowly, the polenta grains absorbing much of the stock and thickening the contents of your pan. You will need to stir frequently, not all the time, but every couple of minutes to make sure it cooks evenly and doesn't catch on the base of the pan.

Simmer for about 30 minutes, or until the polenta grains soften and the mixture is as thick as you would like it to be – remembering that it will continue to cook and thicken when you take it off the heat.

Stir in the parmesan, or pass it around at the table. Serve immediately.

Mamma made a stock every week. What went into it depended on what she had on hand: chicken bones, pieces of chicken, a carrot, celery, a white onion and parsley. Sometimes she would add cheaper cuts of beef to flavour and cook in the broth, which she and my father would then enjoy thinly sliced with mustard and horseradish.

The resulting stock – which we called *brodo* – was strained, the fat skimmed off, and then enjoyed through the week. Mamma would sometimes add small pasta shapes or rice to cook in the broth, but my favourite was a whole egg whisked with a handful of parmesan. We called this pasta *butada* in dialect. The eggs clump together in the broth, making salty, soft mounds of deliciousness. I also love adding a squeeze of lemon to the egg before dropping it in. It is so wholesome and speaks of home and love and was, according to my mother, the perfect medicine for a cold.

Chicken egg-drop soup

STRACCIATELLA

SERVES 4-6

800 g (1 lb 12 oz) chicken
    pieces, including bones
1 small carrot, roughly chopped
1 celery stalk, roughly chopped
½ white onion, peeled
3–4 parsley stalks

To serve
1 egg per person
handful of grated parmesan
    per person
1 teaspoon freshly squeezed
    lemon juice per person

Place the chicken, vegetables and parsley stalks in a large saucepan. Pour in enough water to fully cover the chicken and bring to the boil. Reduce the heat and simmer for at least 2½ hours, skimming off the impurities when it starts to bubble away, and topping up with a little water if needed.

Alternatively, place the chicken, vegetables and parsley stalks in a pressure cooker and cover with water to the maximum level indicated. Following the manufacturer's instructions, cook on high pressure for 45 minutes. Allow the pressure to release slowly for about 30 minutes. When it has finished, carefully release the lid and allow to cool for at least 30 minutes.

Strain off the chicken pieces and vegetables, discarding the bones; the poached chicken meat and vegetables can be eaten as they are or reserved for other uses. Strain the broth through a fine-meshed sieve. Pour into a large container, then cover and place in the fridge overnight.

The next day, skim off and discard the firmer layer of fat that has risen to the top. Your broth is now ready to use. It will keep in a covered glass container in the fridge for up to 1 week, or can be frozen in portions.

To make the soup, heat the desired amount of broth (usually two large ladlefuls per person) in a small saucepan. Add salt to taste. For every serving, beat 1 egg with a handful of parmesan and the lemon juice. Drop it in the warmed soup and cook for a few minutes over medium heat, until lovely eggy pillows form. Serve immediately.

3 tablespoons extra virgin
olive oil

1 white or brown onion, finely
chopped

1 small leek, white and pale
green part only, washed
well, sliced into finger-width
rounds

1 garlic clove, finely chopped

1 carrot, sliced into 5 mm
(¼ inch) rounds

1 celery stalk, cut into 5 mm
(¼ inch) slices

2 all-purpose potatoes, peeled
and cut into 6–8 pieces
each

2 zucchini (courgettes), sliced
into 1 cm (½ inch) rounds

1.25 litres (5 cups) warm
chicken stock (see page 34)
or vegetable broth, or
1.25 litres (5 cups) boiling
water plus a good-quality
stock (bouillon) cube

5–6 parsley stalks, with leaves

4–5 silverbeet (Swiss chard)
stalks, washed well

pearl barley or medium-grain
rice, 1 small handful per
serve (see Note)

basil pesto (page 74), to serve

My mother went through a soup phase that lasted most of her life. When she retired from working in the factory, she made it more often and would give me a giant jar to take home when my daughter, Tamara, and I visited her for Sunday lunch. After my father passed away, she had soup for dinner every night. She said it was one of the reasons she was so long lived.

This was the most frequent version, a sort of 'fridge clean' soup, where whatever vegetables she had on hand would be chopped and dropped in the pot. Like her, I prepare the ingredients as I go, starting with the onion and leek, then the garlic, and after that, the firmest vegetables – carrots, then celery, and so on. She would add a handful of pre-cooked barley or rice at the end, just enough for the bowl she was having that night. A final dollop of basil pesto adds a really lovely touch.

Everyday vegetable soup with basil pesto

MINESTRA DI VERDURA CON PESTO AL BASILICO

Warm the olive oil in a heavy-based saucepan over medium–low heat. Add the onion, leek and a good pinch of salt and saute for about 15 minutes, until the leek is soft.

Next, add the garlic and stir for a minute or two. When fragrant, add the carrot, celery, potato and zucchini, stirring as you add each vegetable. Pour in the stock (or boiling water and stock cube) and add the parsley.

Remove the thickest part of the silverbeet stalks, as well as any damaged bits. Finely chop the stalks and add to the soup. Finely chop the leaves and add them as well. Season with salt and freshly cracked black pepper to taste. Simmer for about 20 minutes, until all the vegetables are cooked through. Remove the parsley stalks and adjust the salt and pepper if needed.

Meanwhile, cook the barley or rice according to the packet instructions and keep warm. Add the barley or rice to individual bowls and ladle the hot soup over. Top each bowl with a large dollop of basil pesto and serve.

NOTE: This soup keeps for 4–5 days without the barley or rice in it. If you are planning on having leftovers, cook only the amount of barley or rice needed for each particular meal, or cook the whole quantity, then refrigerate the leftovers in a separate container and reheat for serving.

PRA DEI GAI

I did not believe that the Pra dei Gai was anything more than a small block of land with a creek behind my mother's home in via Fossabiuba, Mansuè, in the Veneto region of Italy. My uncle used to tease my aunt Clara about it, talking it up so that it became a fancy manicured garden where families got dressed up and would go strolling in the late afternoon, just to be seen. Mamma would describe it as a field where she would play with her brothers and sisters in the years they lived in the Swiss chalet–style home her uncle and father had built. When I visited in 2022, I had no idea if it was still there, or if houses had been built on it. I could not even find it on a map – except, when I looked closely, I noted a network of narrow, winding unpaved roads all called 'via Gai' (Gai Road).

When I started exploring the roads behind what had been the Carli home on foot, I was blown away by what I found: vast fields of land dotted with bales of hay, poplars, plantations of vines, corn, peas and wheat. The Pra dei Gai covers 340 hectares of flood plain from the Livenza River, with a narrow embankment, occasional creek beds, and established alders and willows able to easily survive the occasional flooding. The resultant silt makes the land rich with nutrients. The green wedge extends from the town of Fontanelle to Mansuè and Portobuffolè, and the narrow roads weaving through make it just the place to go bike-riding or walking. It wasn't the manicured lawn my uncle used to tease his wife, Clara, about – but far lovelier.

To find out more about it, I chatted to locals Sergio, Dario and Gino when I was staying in Mansuè to research this book. The name was the first thing I asked about. In Veneto dialect, Pra dei Gai is *prato dei galli* in Italian, which means 'field of roosters.' So how did the name come about? Sergio and Gino both agree that legend has it that the land was sold for some roosters. The exact number of roosters, however, is a point of contention. Was it two or three? They could not reach agreement. Dario tentatively suggested it was a place where roosters went to drink, though quickly admitted he might be wrong. A search on the internet for the origins of the name is also fruitless.

> **My uncle used to tease my aunt Clara about it, talking it up so that it became a fancy manicured garden where families got dressed up and would go strolling in the late afternoon, just to be seen.**

One thing they all agree on is that, in spring, it is a place for picnics. On 25 April, a day of celebration for the Feast of St Mark – and also a national holiday for Liberation Day after the end of World War II – picnic baskets would be packed for a day on the Pra dei Gai, a custom that occurs to this day. Dario tells me frittata (creamy cooked eggs in a pan) is the traditional thing to eat at the picnic. Sergio specifies that it has to be made with salami, and is called *fortaia* in the local dialect: a high-rise, protein-dense, frittata that he called *un piatto forte* – a 'strong' dish of sorts. When asked whether anyone would make it with asparagus or spinach, since these would be in season, a swift 'no' is the reply. I imagine that the use of salami is related not only to the importance of the celebration (after all, meat is not an everyday food for most), but also its timing. Charcuterie-making traditionally happens in December, after a pig has been appropriately fattened – and by the following April, the meats should have cured enough to be ready to eat.

I like to think that Mamma, her parents, her brothers and sisters, cousins and aunts and uncles, would all gather on the Pra dei Gai on this date, walking through the backyard of their home and past the embankment. They would lay down a blanket, unwrap the cloth that covered plates and trays of food, and feast on *fortaia*, bread and fruit under the alders.

Pra dei Gai, Veneto (2022).

In Italy, 25 April is a day of celebration. It is the Feast of St Mark, the patron saint of Venice, as well as Liberation Day, marking Italy's freedom from Nazi-fascism in 1945. In Mamma's home town of Mansuè, a picnic was held on the field near her home, the Pra dei Gai. A favourite dish to make was a frittata/omelette, or as they say in the local dialect, *fortaia*. This has another meaning; the word *forte* means strong, and the traditional *fortaia* made for the picnic is a hearty (or strong) frittata with salami.

My version uses good-quality pork sausage instead of salami – and, although not found in a traditional *fortaia*, a few handfuls of spinach and cheese.

Sausage & spinach frittata
FORTAIA CON SALSICCIA E SPINACI

SERVES 4-6 AS PART OF A PICNIC SPREAD

1 small bunch of English spinach, or 80 g (2¾ oz) frozen spinach
4 eggs
handful of grated parmesan
2 good-quality pork sausages
1 tablespoon extra virgin olive oil
50 g (1¾ oz) Asiago, or your favourite cow's milk melting cheese, finely sliced
finely chopped parsley, for sprinkling

If using fresh spinach, wash the leaves several times in plenty of water and discard the thick stems and any damaged leaves. Blanch briefly in a large saucepan of salted boiling water, then drain. Once cool enough to handle, squeeze the leaves really well to remove the excess moisture, then chop finely. If using frozen spinach, follow the packet instructions to cook on the stovetop or in the microwave; drain well.

Preheat an overhead grill (broiler) to medium–high.

Break the eggs into a large bowl and whisk until well combined. Season with salt and freshly cracked black pepper, add the parmesan and stir until combined.

Remove the skin from the sausages and break the meat into large crumbs. Warm the olive oil in an ovenproof omelette pan or non-stick frying pan. Add the sausage and cook over medium heat, tossing frequently, until the sausage is cooked through.

Scatter the spinach evenly over the sausage and give it a stir. Once well coated in the pan juices, pour in the egg. Reduce the heat to medium–low and cook for about 5 minutes, lifting and tilting the pan regularly so the egg cooks evenly. The edge of the frittata should be starting to firm up, and the centre should still be soft, but not runny.

Lay the cheese slices on top and place the pan under the grill to melt the cheese and firm up the frittata; this will take about 5 minutes.

Slide the frittata out of the frying pan, onto a chopping board. Grind some black pepper over and sprinkle with the parsley. Allow to cool for a few minutes, then slice into wedges. Serve warm, or at room temperature.

Italians are known for eating bread at every meal. My uncle Fidenzio in particular was a big bread eater, and would follow a mouthful of food with a bite of bread. When going to a restaurant, my aunt Alba would pack a few rosettes of bread in her handbag, just in case the restaurant didn't serve it in sufficient quantities for my uncle.

Bread-making was not Mamma's strongest point, my father not eating nearly as much bread as my uncle, though she made a very good focaccia using milk rather than water. While lovely on its own, it was the most delicious accompaniment to cold cuts and cheeses. I have used my dear friend Verdiana's suggestions to tweak Mamma's handwritten recipe. Thank you, Verdiana.

Focaccia with milk

FOCACCIA MORBIDA CON IL LATTE

**SERVES 6-8;
MY HUSBAND AND I ATE IT ALL IN ONE MEAL THE FIRST TIME I MADE IT!**

500 g (1 lb 2 oz) plain (all-purpose) flour, plus extra for dusting
2 teaspoons (7 g) instant dried yeast
½ teaspoon sugar
375 ml (1½ cups) milk
2 tablespoons extra virgin olive oil
1 teaspoon fine sea salt

For the emulsion
2 tablespoons extra virgin olive oil
3 tablespoons hot water
1 scant teaspoon coarse sea salt or salt flakes

Place the flour, yeast and sugar in a large wide bowl and whisk to combine. Make a well in the centre.

Warm the milk so it is tepid; combine with the olive oil and pour into the flour well. Stir with a spoon to combine, then add the salt. Bring the dough together as much as you can with the spoon – it will be quite shaggy and soft. Knead briefly using lightly floured hands, so the dough is cohesive and relatively homogenous, then gently shape it into a loose ball.

Place the dough in a large lightly oiled bowl. Cover and set aside in a warm spot for about 3 hours, until doubled in size (the oven with the light turned on works well if your kitchen is cold).

Using your fingertips, oil the base and sides of a rimmed baking tray. My tray measures 30 cm × 20 cm (12 inches × 10 inches), with a rim height of 3 cm (1¼ inches). Using oiled hands, lift the dough into the tray, then spread it out to cover the base of the tray, using your fingertips to push it towards the edges. Cover and allow to rest in a warm spot for another 45 minutes.

Preheat the oven to 200°C (400°F) fan-forced.

Prepare the emulsion by mixing the olive oil and hot water. Drizzle over the top of the focaccia. Using your fingertips, make indentations in the dough, so that the emulsion pools in them. Sprinkle the salt flakes over the focaccia.

Bake for 20–25 minutes, or until the top of the focaccia is golden.

The focaccia is best eaten within a day of making. If you have any left after that, make toasties in a sandwich press with the focaccia sliced through the middle.

PASTA & RICE

1. **Spaghetti with oven-roasted tomato pesto**
2. **Fettuccine with veal & mushroom ragù**
3. **Cannelloni with ricotta, spinach & oven-roasted tomatoes**
4. **Rice, peas & prosciutto**
5. **Parmesan risotto**
6. **Risotto with sausage & tomatoes**

Pesto is most frequently associated with basil (see page 74), but can be made with many other ingredients. In Italian, the word pesto means an amalgam of ingredients that are bashed together. This is my mother's version of red pesto, made with homemade oven-roasted tomatoes. Using the olive oil the roasted tomatoes are stored in gives the pesto a deep, rich tomato flavour; alternatively, use store-bought sun-dried tomatoes and excellent extra virgin olive oil. You can easily double or triple the pesto recipe if you need a greater quantity. It is also lovely as a spread on crusty bread.

Spaghetti with oven-roasted tomato pesto

SPAGHETTI AL PESTO ROSSO

SERVES 2

200–250 g (7–9 oz) spaghetti, depending on your appetite

Tomato pesto
40 g (1½ oz) oven-roasted tomatoes (see page 68)
25 g (1 oz) pitted black olives
20 g (¾ oz) pine nuts, toasted
1 small garlic clove, roughly chopped
25 g (¼ cup) grated parmesan
1 tablespoon parsley leaves
80 ml (⅓ cup) extra virgin olive oil

To serve
4–8 oven-roasted tomatoes, cut into long strips
chopped parsley, for scattering
extra virgin olive oil, for drizzling
grated parmesan, for sprinkling

Start by making the pesto. If using larger oven-roasted tomatoes, roughly chop them before you begin. Place the tomato in a small food processor with the remaining pesto ingredients and pulse until the desired consistency is achieved. Scrape into a large bowl. Add the extra oven-roasted tomato strips and season with salt to taste.

Cook the spaghetti in a large saucepan of salted boiling water, following the packet instructions, until al dente. Drain the spaghetti, reserving a little of the pasta water, and add to the bowl of pesto. Stir well with a large fork or tongs until the pesto coats the spaghetti, adding a little reserved pasta water (or some extra virgin olive oil) to loosen if needed.

Pile the spaghetti onto two warmed plates. Scatter with extra parsley, anoint with more olive oil and finish with a sprinkling of parmesan.

Mamma always had a batch of ragù – or sugo, as we also called it – in the fridge. She would make it weekly to last for several meals and be eaten with pasta, risotto, or simply thick slices of bread for dunking. In our house, this version with veal was made less commonly than in the kitchens of northern Italy, because veal is harder to find in Australia. As an alternative, you could use lean pork or yearling beef. The joy of this dish is the combination of the slow-cooked meat and the earthy taste of the mushrooms.

Fettuccine with veal & mushroom ragù

FETTUCCINE CON SUGO DI VITELLO E FUNGHI

SERVES 4-6

10 g (¼ oz) dried porcini mushrooms
2 tablespoons extra virgin olive oil, plus extra for drizzling
40 g (1½ oz) butter
1 white onion, finely diced
1 small carrot, finely diced
1 small celery stalk, finely diced
40 g (1½ oz) pancetta, finely diced
1 garlic clove, finely diced
600 g (1 lb 5 oz) veal fillet slices, cut into 1 cm (½ inch) strips
80 ml (⅓ cup) dry white wine
2 teaspoons tomato paste (concentrated purée)
350 g (12½ oz) Swiss brown mushrooms, sliced
1 stem of sage leaves
400–600 g (14 oz–1 lb 5 oz) fettuccine
grated parmesan, for sprinkling

Place the dried mushrooms in a small bowl and cover with hot (not boiling) water. Allow to soak for about 20 minutes to reconstitute. Strain the water and reserve.

Warm the olive oil and butter in a large heavy-based saucepan over medium–low heat. When the butter has melted, add the onion, carrot, celery and pancetta and saute for about 20 minutes, until the vegetables have softened and the pancetta has rendered its fat. Add the garlic and cook for a few minutes, until fragrant. Add the veal strips and turn up the heat to high, stirring frequently for a few minutes to brown them.

Stir in the wine. After a few minutes, when most of the liquid has evaporated, reduce the heat to medium and stir in the tomato paste. Add the Swiss brown mushrooms, strained dried porcini and their soaking water, the sage leaves and 125 ml (½ cup) of water. Stir well, then season with salt and freshly cracked black pepper to taste.

Reduce the heat to low. Cover and simmer for about 1½ hours, stirring occasionally. If the ragù looks a bit dry, add another 60 ml (¼ cup) of water. It is ready when the meat is falling apart and the ragù tastes delicious! Remove the sage leaves and adjust for salt.

Cook the fettuccine in a large saucepan of salted boiling water, following the packet instructions, until al dente.

Drain the fettuccine and place in a large bowl. Drizzle on a little extra virgin olive oil to loosen the pasta, stir through and then top with the ragù. Serve with the grated parmesan.

Any leftover ragù will keep in a covered ceramic container in the fridge for up to a week.

MEMORIES OF NONNA'S TABLE
by Claire Davie, Livia's eldest grandchild

*I*xe qua, ti pol butar la pasta! My nonno's voice was typically the first thing we'd hear as we approached the front door, advising Nonna of our arrival and signalling that the pasta could be thrown into the standby pot of water. There was an unwritten rule that if we were going to be late we should make a courtesy phone call, because Nonna was particular about timing meals so that we'd be eating the *primo piatto* almost as soon as we arrived. As with many Italians of their era, they had a discomfort with the notion of standing around drinking on an empty stomach, preferring to only pour a welcome glass of vino for adults once plates were before us.

We'd cross the threshold and pass the 1970s home bar, with its arched shelving, red-brick wallpaper and Laminex counter, to reach the kitchen. My earliest memories of it recall a mission-brown room with splashes of orange dominated by a circular table, but following the early-1990s installation of a box window and pastel-blue paint job, it became airy and bright. In both incarnations, the kitchen was always fastidiously clean, swept to within an inch of its life.

If we were having gnocchi (my favourite), we'd arrive to see hundreds of gnocchi that had been rolled with a fork, sitting in neat rows on trays, awaiting the pot. *Primo piatto* was usually pasta, risotto or a soup – either a shimmering bowl of *brodo* or, if it was winter, a hearty serve of *jota* (the sauerkraut and bean soup of their childhoods).

The *secondo piatto* was generally centred around meat or fish – sometimes, if we were lucky, it would be *calamari fritti* (despite Nonna's worry about how it would dirty the stovetop) or seafood skewers, cooked on the outdoor barbecue. When, as often was the case, ingredients had come from Nonno's extensive vegetable garden, he'd show off about how fresh they were, bragging that they had still been growing just an hour ago. The soundtrack would be opera, mid-century crooners like Sinatra and Bennett, or older Italian love songs.

> **"**
> **Ingredients had come from Nonno's extensive vegetable garden, he'd show off about how fresh they were, bragging that they had still been growing just an hour ago.**

In the pause between main course and dessert, Nonna would do the dishes, politely refusing assistance because she didn't trust us to wash them properly. As children, we would play in the home bar – writing drinks lists, pouring imaginary cocktails and making the grown-ups pay for them with Monopoly money – or muck around in the dining room, driving toy vehicles through the thick brown-and-cream shag pile carpet (sadly lost to history when the dining room was later refurbished with floorboards). Of the *dolci* Nonna would serve us, our favourites were *giorno e notte* (marble cake), *crostoli* and, above all, her *fritole* (Venetian doughnuts).

Like most grandmothers, Nonna loved spoiling her grandchildren, and this would manifest in personalised ways at her table. Knowing that my brother loved cucumbers, she would set out a saucer with peeled cucumber slices next to his dinner plate. My sister's love of balsamic vinegar was indulged by a tiny dish of the stuff, for bread dunking. My cousin Tamara's love of avocado meant she got her own half in a small bowl. And there was always a packet of Tim Tam chocolate biscuits in the fridge to hand out to her grandchildren as we kissed her goodbye.

Cannelloni were a regular feature of Sunday family lunches. The vegetarian version was made with our homemade passata, which was stored in brown beer bottles in the cellar directly under the kitchen and one would occasionally explode as we were sitting down to a meal. My father would sigh, knowing exactly what had happened, and make his way downstairs to find passata everywhere. It was messy, but luckily did not happen often.

Cannelloni are terrific when entertaining, as you can assemble them ahead in the baking dish, cover and pop in the fridge for half a day. Just remember to bring the dish to room temperature before placing in the oven.

Cannelloni with ricotta, spinach & oven-roasted tomatoes

CANNELLONI RIPIENI DELLA MAMMA

To make the pasta, place the flour on your work surface in a mound and make a well in the centre. Crack the eggs into the well and start whisking the liquid gently with a fork, incorporating a bit of flour at the same time. When the mixture becomes too thick to use the fork, use your fingertips to work the wet ingredients into the dry ingredients until a ball of dough forms. You may need to add a bit of water/flour to get the right consistency. Knead for about 10 minutes, until smooth and elastic. Cover and allow to rest for at least 30 minutes.

Dust your work surface with more flour. Cut off half the dough and keep the rest covered.

Roll the first half of the dough out with a rolling pin until it is thin enough to go through the widest setting of your pasta machine. Thread it through the rollers of the machine, turning the handle and allowing the pasta sheet to drop from the machine. Fold the thinned sheet in half, dust with flour if sticky, and give it a quarter turn before threading it through the machine again. Repeat as many times as needed to make the dough lose much of its stretch (usually five or six times). Try to keep the dough in a rectangular shape; you may need to use the rolling pin to help you shape it.

SERVES 4 AS A FIRST COURSE

For the pasta
200 g (7 oz) 00 pasta flour, plus
    extra for dusting
2 large eggs, at room
    temperature

Tomato sugo
1 generous tablespoon extra
    virgin olive oil
½ brown or white onion, finely
    chopped
600 g (1 lb 5 oz) good-quality
    tomato passata (pureed
    tomatoes)
generous pinch of dried
    oregano

Filling
1 big bunch of English spinach,
    or 250 g (9 oz) frozen
    spinach
1 tablespoon extra virgin
    olive oil
1 garlic clove, finely chopped
280 g (10 oz) ricotta, drained
80 g (2¾ oz) oven-roasted
    tomatoes (see page 68),
    or store-bought sun-dried
    tomatoes
80 g (2¾ oz) parmesan, grated

For topping
80 g (2¾ oz) mozzarella or
    scamorza bianca, sliced

Once the dough has become firm and glossy, start turning the dial of the machine so the rollers are closer together, rolling the dough thinner each time, once through each setting. You no longer need to turn the dough. Dust the pasta sheets with flour if sticky. Continue until your pasta is quite thin – usually the second-thinnest setting of your machine. Cut the pasta into 10 cm (4 inch) squares, making 12 to 14 squares.

Roll out and cut the remaining dough half in the same way.

Bring a large saucepan of salted water to the boil. Working in batches, cook the pasta squares for a few minutes, until cooked, using tongs to carefully remove the pasta to a colander. Run under cold water to stop the cooking process, then drain. Place the pasta squares in a single layer on a clean tea towel; pat dry with another tea towel.

To make the tomato sugo, warm the olive oil in a saucepan. Add the onion, sprinkle with a good pinch of salt and saute for 10 minutes over low heat or until well softened. Stir in the passata, oregano and salt to taste. Cover and simmer for another 15 minutes or so. The sugo should be quite runny; if it isn't, add about 125 ml (½ cup) of water during cooking. You will have more sugo than you need for this recipe; seal the remainder in a large glass jar in the fridge and use within a week.

To make the filling, remove the stalks and any damaged leaves from the fresh spinach and wash the leaves several times to remove any soil. Place a large saucepan on the stovetop over medium–high heat. Using tongs, add the drained spinach leaves to the pan and push them down until they wilt with the heat. Once wilted, remove and place in a colander to drain. Finely chop and set aside. (If using frozen spinach, follow the packet instructions to cook on the stovetop or in the microwave; drain well.)

Warm the olive oil and garlic in a small frying pan over medium heat. Once the garlic becomes fragrant, add the spinach and cook for a few minutes, until well infused with the garlic and oil. Season with salt to taste and set aside.

Beat the ricotta in a bowl with a fork until smooth and spreadable.

Place the oven-roasted tomatoes in a mini food processor and pulse until a paste forms, adding a little of their olive oil if needed. Alternatively, you can finely chop them.

To assemble the cannelloni, spread a few tablespoons of the tomato sugo in the base of a baking dish; the one I use is 26 cm (10¼ inch) square.

Smear ½ teaspoon of the roasted tomato paste on three-quarters of a pasta square, leaving a clear edge on one side. Top with 1½ teaspoons of the ricotta and a sprinkling of parmesan, reserving half the parmesan for the topping. Lastly, add a heaped teaspoon of spinach, spreading it over the cheeses. Add a grinding of black pepper, then roll up fairly tightly towards the free edge of the pasta and place in the baking dish.

Repeat until you have used up all the pasta squares and all the filling ingredients (except the reserved parmesan).

Pour about 375 ml (1½ cups) of the tomato sugo over the cannelloni; the pasta rolls should be just covered. If they aren't, add a bit more sugo (or water). Cover with the mozzarella slices, then sprinkle with the reserved parmesan. (You can cover the dish and refrigerate at this point, then bring it back to room temperature before proceeding.)

When ready to bake, preheat the oven to 180°C (350°F) fan-forced.

Bake the cannelloni on the top shelf of your oven for 20–25 minutes, until the rolls are warmed through and the cheese has melted and is turning golden. Remove from the oven and allow to rest for about 10 minutes before serving.

Leftovers will keep in a covered container in the fridge for a day and can be gently reheated in the microwave.

On the General Greeley, travelling to Australia (1950).

Mamma was open to discovering different ways of enjoying favourite dishes, and loved it when I showed her how to place a slice of very thin prosciutto over cooked risotto, after learning it from my friend Enrica in Venice. The prosciutto melts and softens ever so slightly, forming a deliciously salty film over the risotto. It is especially lovely with *risi e bisi* (rice and peas), the soupy risotto that is typical of the Veneto region.

I love adding leftover parmesan crusts to the risotto, as they impart a deliciously cheesy saltiness. When there is only the crust remaining from a block of parmesan, I scrape any paint or wax from the rind, cut it into bite-sized chunks and store it in a sealed container in the freezer, ready to use in soups and risottos.

Rice, peas & prosciutto
RISI E BISI CON PROSCIUTTO

SERVES 4

2 tablespoons extra virgin olive oil

45 g (1½ oz) unsalted butter

½ brown or white onion, finely diced

1.25–1.5 litres (5–6 cups) good-quality chicken stock

320 g (11½ oz) carnaroli, vialone nano or arborio rice

60 ml (¼ cup) dry white wine

40 g (1½ oz) parmesan crusts (optional)

280 g (10 oz) frozen peas

60 g (2 oz) parmesan, grated

1 tablespoon finely chopped parsley

4–8 very thin slices room-temperature prosciutto, cut into long strips

Warm the olive oil and 15 g (½ oz) of the butter in a large saucepan. Add the onion and saute over medium–low heat for 12 minutes, stirring occasionally, until softened and translucent. Don't let it turn brown.

Meanwhile, pour the stock into a separate saucepan and bring to the boil. Reduce the heat and let it simmer while you make the risotto. Also have some boiling water on hand in case you need extra liquid.

Add the rice to the sauteed onion and toast for a few minutes, until it takes on a slightly golden hue. Increase the heat and add the wine, stirring with a wooden spoon so the rice doesn't stick or burn. Once that has evaporated, add a ladleful of the stock and reduce the heat to medium–low. Toss in the parmesan crusts, if using (straight from the freezer is fine). Allow to slowly bubble away, stirring every minute or so, to ensure the rice doesn't stick to the base, adding more stock as the previous lot is absorbed. After a couple of minutes, add the peas.

The rice will take 14–18 minutes in total to cook, depending on the type you use (arborio takes less time). Texture is the best indicator for determining when it is ready, so make sure you taste it – the rice should feel slightly firm when you bite into it, and be not quite cooked. The mixture should be a bit soupier than a regular risotto. Season with salt.

Remove from the heat; the rice will continue to cook. Add the remaining 30 g (1 oz) of butter, stir well and cover. After a minute, add the grated parmesan, the parsley and some freshly cracked black pepper, stirring well. Cover and leave to rest for another few minutes. Ladle into shallow serving bowls, top with the prosciutto strips and serve immediately.

When I look back on the photos of my lunches with Mamma in the last eight years of her life, I realise risotto featured prominently, much more than pasta. When you are cooking for one, it does not make sense to go to the effort of making risotto, so the children and grandchildren had the benefit of eating a lot of risotto during these years.

You can think of the recipe below as a basic risotto recipe, which you can use with the braises in the Mostly Vegetables chapter of this book.

For risotto, you need to use a rice variety that retains some bite after 15–18 minutes of slow-absorption cooking. Arborio is the most readily available, but look for the vialone nano or carnaroli varieties, which are superior, as they retain more structure (bite) than arborio.

Parmesan risotto

RISOTTO AL PARMIGIANO

SERVES 4

2 tablespoons extra virgin olive oil
45 g (1½ oz) unsalted butter
½ brown or white onion, finely diced
1.25 litres (5 cups) good-quality chicken stock
320 g (11½ oz) carnaroli, vialone nano or arborio rice
60 ml (¼ cup) dry white wine
40 g (1½ oz) parmesan crusts (optional)
50 g (½ cup) grated parmesan, plus extra to serve

Warm the olive oil and 15 g (½ oz) of the butter in a large saucepan. Add the onion and saute over medium–low heat for 12 minutes, stirring occasionally, until softened and translucent. Don't let it turn brown.

Meanwhile, pour the stock into a seprate saucepan and bring to the boil. Reduce the heat and let it simmer while you make the risotto. Also have some boiling water on hand in case you need extra liquid.

Add the rice to the sauteed onion and toast for a few minutes, until it takes on a slightly golden hue. Increase the heat and add the wine, stirring with a wooden spoon so the rice doesn't stick or burn. Once that has evaporated, add a ladleful of the hot stock and reduce the heat to medium–low. Toss in the parmesan crusts, if using. Allow to slowly bubble away, stirring every minute or so, to ensure the rice doesn't stick to the base and cooks evenly, adding more stock as the previous lot is absorbed.

The rice will take about 14–18 minutes in total to cook, depending on the type you use (arborio takes less time). Texture is the best indicator for determining when it is ready, so make sure you taste it – the rice should feel slightly firm when you bite into it, and be not quite cooked. Season with salt to taste.

Remove from the heat; the rice will continue to cook. Add the remaining 30 g (1 oz) butter, stir well and cover. After a minute, add the parmesan, stir well and cover. It will be lovely and creamy by now. Serve after a couple of minutes, with extra parmesan and a grinding of black pepper.

I introduced Mamma to the idea of cooking risotto directly in passata when she was living alone after my father had passed. She was open to new tricks in the kitchen well into her 80s and loved the simplicity of it. You can leave out the sausages in this dish to turn it into a simple vegetarian tomato risotto.

Risotto with sausage & tomatoes

RISOTTO AL POMODORO CON SALSICCIA

SERVES 2

440 g (15½ oz) tomato passata (pureed tomatoes), or crushed tomatoes

2 tablespoons extra virgin olive oil, plus extra for pan-frying

½ small brown or white onion

2 good-quality pork and fennel sausages

160 g (5½ oz) carnaroli, vialone nano or arborio rice

60 ml (¼ cup) dry white wine

4–6 pieces parmesan crust (optional)

50 g (1¾ oz) butter

50 g (½ cup) grated parmesan, plus extra to serve

Pour the passata into a saucepan and stir in 250 ml (1 cup) of water. Allow to slowly come to the boil. You will be using this as the stock for your risotto.

Warm the olive oil in a large saucepan. Add the onion and saute over medium–low heat for 12 minutes, stirring occasionally, until softened and translucent. Don't let it turn brown.

While the onion is cooking, pan-fry the sausages. Cut them into chunks and place in a small frying pan with a splash of olive oil. Cook over medium heat, turning occasionally so the sausage pieces cook evenly. Fry for about 8 minutes in total; it doesn't matter if they aren't completely cooked through as they'll continue to cook in the risotto.

Back to the risotto. Once the onion has been sauteed, add the rice and toast for a few minutes, until it takes on a slightly golden hue. Increase the heat and add the wine, stirring with a wooden spoon so the rice doesn't stick or burn. Once that has evaporated, add a ladleful of the hot passata stock and reduce the heat to medium–low. Toss in the parmesan crusts, if using. Allow to slowly bubble away, stirring every minute or so, so that the rice doesn't stick to the base and cooks evenly, adding more passata stock as the previous lot is absorbed. Once the sausages are done, toss them into the risotto too.

The rice will take about 14–18 minutes in total to cook, depending on the type you use (arborio takes less time). Texture is the best indicator for determining when it is ready, so make sure you taste it – the rice should feel slightly firm when you bite into it, and be not quite cooked. Season with salt to taste and add a good grinding of black pepper.

Remove from the heat; the rice will continue to cook. Add the butter, stir well and cover. After a minute, add the parmesan, stir well and cover.

Serve after a couple of minutes, with extra parmesan.

MOSTLY VEGETABLES

1. Oven-roasted tomatoes preserved in olive oil
2. Julius Caesar salad
3. Potato salad with basil pesto
4. Green beans & tomatoes
5. Twice-cooked spinach with parmesan & lemon
6. Red pepper braise
7. Zucchini with prosciutto
8. Brussels sprouts with pancetta
9. Braised mushrooms
10. Peperonata with zucchini & red pepper
11. Peperonata with eggplant & tomato
12. Potatoes & silverbeet
13. Peas & sausages
14. Potato & tomato stew
15. Stuffed tomatoes
16. Crepes with spinach & fontina

Each year, at the end of summer, the top shelf of Mamma's fridge would be laden with jars of her basil pesto and oven-dried tomatoes to last through until the next summer. Not that they ever lasted that long. When my daughter, Tamara, and I went over for lunch, invariably we were gifted a jar of one or the other as we were leaving – and my father would check my basket just to make sure Mamma had not given me more than one jar. The tomatoes and basil had been grown in his vegetable garden, so he felt some ownership on how much could be gifted at any one time!

The tomatoes were really special. Mamma would remove all the seeds before drying them in the oven at low temperature to the point where they were still fleshy and sweet. And after a week, the oil in which they were preserved was divine and tomatoey.

In peak season I usually buy 3–4 kilos (6 lb 10 oz–8 lb 13 oz) of tomatoes from the market, when they are ripe and maybe slightly drying out naturally, and being sold at a fraction of the usual cost. They take a bit of time to prepare – but put on a good podcast or some music, and invite a friend to help you, and you'll be rewarded with jars of tomatoes that taste like a ray of summer sunshine.

The recipe below uses only a kilo of tomatoes, but you can easily scale up the recipe to preserve a larger batch.

Oven-roasted tomatoes preserved in olive oil

POMODORI SECCHI SOTT'OLIO

MAKES 1 × 500 ML (17 FL OZ) JAR

1 kg (2 lb 3 oz) small ripe tasty
   tomatoes
1½ teaspoons sea salt
dried oregano (ideally whole
   sprigs)
1 garlic clove, peeled and sliced
   (optional – see Note)
good-quality extra virgin olive
   oil, for covering

Preheat the oven to 100°C (210°F) fan-forced. Line a large baking tray with baking paper.

Check over the tomatoes and discard any that are too soft or past their best. Wash and thoroughly dry the tomatoes. Cut them in half, then remove the core and scoop out the seeds. Place on the baking tray, cut side up, without crowding them on the tray; depending on the size of your tray, you may need to use a second lined baking tray. Sprinkle the sea salt over the tomatoes.

Roast the tomatoes for 1–½ hours, until the edges are dry, but the centre is still fleshy. The exact roasting time will depend on the size and quality of your tomatoes. Remove from the oven and place the baking tray on a wire rack to cool.

Turn the oven temperature down to 80°C (175°F). While the roasted tomatoes are cooling, wash a 500 ml (17 fl oz) glass jar, and its lid, in hot soapy water and rinse well. Place the upturned jar and lid in the oven to dry for 20 minutes. Remove from the oven and leave until cool enough to handle.

Using tongs, place the roasted tomatoes in the warm jar, adding a couple of oregano sprigs and the garlic, if using, as you go, and leaving a space of about 5 mm (¼ inch) at the top of the jar. Cover the tomatoes with olive oil and seal the jar.

Store the jar in the fridge and use within 3–4 months. The tomatoes are wonderful as part of an antipasto platter, on their own with crusty bread, or with sliced buffalo mozzarella and a bit of the olive oil from the jar drizzled on top. Mamma would also finely chop them and stir through freshly cooked pasta with a good dash of the olive oil and some grated parmesan for a simple lunch, or turn them into a red pesto, based on the recipe on page 48.

NOTE: Only add the garlic if you're intending to use the tomatoes within a month, as the garlic does not keep well.

Opposite: Outside the newly built house in Station Street, Box Hill South, Melbourne (1954).
This page: Travelling to Italy on the Lloyd Triestino ship 'Marconi' (1972).

In the 1990s my parents discovered an Italian restaurant on the Mornington Peninsula called Giulio Cesare (as in Julius Caesar, the legendary Roman Emperor). We would go there for birthdays and other celebrations. The restaurant's specialities were seafood, a terrific garlic focaccia and the eponymous salad, which they called *Insalata Giulio Cesare* - rather than Caesar salad, which was named after an Italian-American chef. My parents loved it so much they were determined to recreate it at home. Papà even purchased Tabasco, which had never before been seen in the house, to make the recipe the way they did at the restaurant. This is such a delicious old-school salad, it needs to make a comeback!

Julius Caesar salad

INSALATA GIULIO CESARE

SERVES 4

3 garlic cloves, unpeeled
2–3 slices white bread
50 g (1¾ oz) thin pancetta
    slices, cut into strips
1 cos (romaine) lettuce, leaves
    separated
30 g (1 oz) parmesan, shaved

Anchovy mayonnaise
2 egg yolks
1 teaspoon white wine vinegar,
    plus a little extra if needed
125 ml (½ cup) mild olive oil
    or grapeseed oil
4 anchovy fillets, finely chopped
a few drops of Tabasco sauce

Preheat the oven to 180°C (350°F) fan-forced. Place two of the garlic cloves on a baking tray and roast for 20 minutes, or until the garlic is soft.

Turn the oven down to 100°C (210°F). Cut the third garlic clove in half and rub the cut sides over the bread slices. Cut the bread into cubes, place on the baking tray and bake for 5–10 minutes, until the bread croutons start to dry out and take on a bit of colour. Set aside.

Place the pancetta on a sheet of foil under an oven grill (broiler) preheated to medium–high, and grill until the pancetta starts releasing its fat and turns a deep pink. Keep an eye on it, so the edges don't burn – it should take no more than 5 minutes if the slices are thin. The pancetta will be a bit soft when hot, but will crisp up as it cools. Set aside.

Wash and spin-dry the lettuce leaves, discarding any damaged ones. Chop or tear the leaves into large pieces and place in a mixing bowl.

To make the mayonnaise, place the egg yolks and vinegar in a tall narrow container. Using a stick blender or electric whisk, beat at low speed, then increase the speed to high and drizzle in the olive oil in a thin steady stream. The mayonnaise should thicken as you add more oil. Squeeze the roasted garlic cloves into the mayonnaise, add the anchovy fillets and give it a light whisk until well incorporated. The mayonnaise should be quite thick. Add salt, if needed, then thin the mayonnaise with a little extra vinegar so that the dressing is pourable and tastes balanced. Add Tabasco, to taste.

Pour half the dressing over the lettuce. Toss until the leaves are well coated. Transfer to a serving bowl, then scatter with the croutons, parmesan and crispy pancetta. Drizzle the remaining dressing over the top and serve immediately.

Basil pesto is a wonderful thing. Mamma always had jars in the fridge, made with beautifully fresh basil grown in the garden. I tend to make a large jar at a time, religiously using a mortar and pestle – though Mamma used a food processor and insisted it was okay. This pesto is not only marvellous as a sauce for pasta, but as a spread on bread, in a sandwich, and to dollop on soup. I also love turning it into a runnier salad dressing, especially with potatoes.

Potato salad with basil pesto

INSALATA DI PATATE CON PESTO AL BASILICO

SERVES 4-6

750 g (1 lb 11 oz) boiling
   potatoes
1–3 tablespoons basil pesto
   (see below)
1 tablespoon extra virgin
   olive oil
2 teaspoons white wine vinegar,
   plus extra if needed
2 tablespoons pine nuts,
   toasted
basil leaves, to serve (optional)

Basil pesto
1 bunch of basil, about 70 g
   (2½ oz), leaves picked
1 small garlic clove, roughly
   chopped
80 ml (⅓ cup) extra virgin olive
   oil, plus extra if needed
30 g (1 oz) pine nuts, toasted
50 g (½ cup) grated parmesan

Peel the potatoes and chop to the desired size; I like them pretty chunky. Place in a saucepan of cold water, add salt to taste and bring to the boil. Cook for 10–15 minutes, until the potatoes can be pierced with a fork, but are not falling apart. Drain, then allow to cool to room temperature (see Note).

To make the pesto, place the basil leaves and garlic in a large mortar with a pinch of sea salt. Start pounding the basil with the pestle. Once the leaves have broken down, drizzle in the olive oil, a little at a time, until it becomes creamy. It may seem a little runny, but that's normal at this stage. Add the pine nuts, pounding until they break apart. Lastly, using a spoon or a spatula, stir in the parmesan, a little at a time. Add sea salt to taste. If not using the pesto immediately, place in a clean lidded jar, cover with extra olive oil and seal. Place in the fridge and use within a week. (If storing the pesto for longer than that, use a sterilised jar, remember to cover well with oil, keep in the fridge and use within 1 month.)

To make the dressing, place 1–3 tablespoons of the basil pesto in a small jar with the olive oil and vinegar. Put the lid on the jar and give it a good shake to combine. Taste and adjust the balance of flavours, adding more vinegar or salt if needed.

Place the cooled potatoes in a serving bowl and carefully stir the dressing through. Scatter with the pine nuts and extra basil, if using, and serve.

NOTE: If the potatoes are still warm when the dressing is stirred through, the basil in the pesto will go dark!

This page: Livia and Nello's wedding, Monfalcone (August, 1948).

Opposite: Christmas on the Mornington Peninsula, Melbourne (2018).

My father had an extensive vegetable garden at our house in Vermont South: beans, tomatoes, zucchini (courgettes), garlic, silverbeet (Swiss chard) and other leafy greens. He would use wooden stakes to help support the tomatoes and beans, hammering them into the soil with a large rubber mallet, and tying them with scraps of Mamma's fabrics or coloured binding. They gave a colourful and rather Italian look to our backyard. The beans were planted two deep on the perimeter of the block, next to the fence, and grew to about 2 metres (6 feet) tall, forming a deep, tall wall of green. I remember being sent out to the garden to collect what would turn into dinner and seeing no beans, but then reaching with my whole arm through that deep wall of green to find the prize: large beans that were ready to pick, right by the fence.

This is a very simple dish and was one of our favourites. I often use it as a pasta sauce.

Green beans & tomatoes

FAGIOLINI E POMODORI

SERVES 3–4

400 g (14 oz) green beans
3 tomatoes, about 400 g (14 oz)
    (see Note)
2 tablespoons extra virgin
    olive oil
½ large brown or white onion,
    finely diced
1 garlic clove, finely diced
pinch of chilli flakes or chilli
    powder
chopped parsley, to serve

Top and tail the beans, then cut them in half, or into thirds if large. Set aside.

Bring a saucepan of water to the boil. Gently plunge the tomatoes in the water. Once the water comes back to the boil (a minute or less), remove the tomatoes with a large slotted spoon. Peel the skin off. Roughly chop the flesh and remove the seeds.

Warm the olive oil in a frying pan or saucepan over medium heat. Add the onion and saute for about 10 minutes, until soft and translucent. Add the garlic. After a minute or two, when fragrant, add the beans, tomatoes, chilli and about 125 ml (½ cup) of water. Season with salt to taste and bring to a simmer.

Cover the pan, reduce the heat to low and simmer for about 30 minutes, until the beans are cooked to your liking. Remove the lid for the last 5 minutes if there is too much liquid – though you might like to leave the sauce runnier if serving with pasta.

Season with more salt if needed, and scatter with parsley before serving.

NOTE: Instead of fresh tomatoes, you could also use a 400 g (14 oz) tin of peeled tomatoes and omit the boiling step.

This is more of a cooking method than a recipe and can be used for more robust leafy greens such as kale, chicory greens or silverbeet (Swiss chard). The greens are initially boiled or steamed, then cooked again (*ripassati*) in olive oil and garlic.

Twice-cooked spinach with parmesan & lemon

SPINACI RIPASSATI CON PARMIGIANO E LIMONE

SERVES 3-4

1-2 large bunches of English spinach
2 tablespoons extra virgin olive oil, approximately
1 garlic clove, finely chopped
a squeeze of lemon juice
30 g (1 oz) parmesan, shaved or coarsely grated

Wash the spinach several times in plenty of water until it drains clean. Remove any damaged leaves and thick stems. Allow the leaves to drain.

Place a large saucepan over medium–high heat. Add the spinach leaves and allow to wilt, using tongs to help push them down; you may need to wilt them in batches.

Remove from the heat. Drain the spinach, reserving all the liquid and any remaining water in the pan as a good-quality vegetable stock to use in other recipes.

Warm the olive oil in a large frying pan over medium heat, adding a little extra if you have a lot of spinach. Add the garlic. After a minute or two, when fragrant, add the wilted spinach, stirring it into the warmed oil and garlic until the spinach is warmed through and well infused. Season with salt to taste.

Serve warm, sprinkled with lemon juice and freshly cracked black pepper, and scattered with parmesan.

This is another version of my mother's peperonata. When warm, it can be served as a side dish to grilled fish, chicken or beef. At room temperature, it is lovely as part of an antipasto platter, served on bread or just with a firm cheese. If you leave the vinegar out, you can also use it as a sauce for pasta.

Red pepper braise

PEPERONI ROSSI

SERVES 3 IN A PASTA SAUCE, OR 6-8 AS PART OF AN ANTIPASTO PLATTER

1 red onion, about 200 g (7 oz)
2 red bell peppers (capsicums), about 450 g (1 lb) in total
3 tablespoons extra virgin olive oil
3 tablespoons tomato passata (pureed tomatoes)
a good pinch of chilli powder
2 tablespoons red wine vinegar

Peel the onion and cut into fine segments. Cut off and discard the red pepper stems. Cut the peppers in half and remove the seeds and membranes. Cut the flesh into thin strips; I like them to be about the same length as the onion segments.

Warm the olive oil in a large frying pan over medium–high heat. Add the onion and a good pinch of salt. Cook for about 5 minutes, stirring frequently, until the onion starts to colour around the edges. Add the red pepper strips to warm through, then stir in the passata and bring to a simmer.

Reduce the heat to medium–low and stir in the chilli. Cover and simmer for about 20 minutes, stirring occasionally, until the red pepper has softened and started to meld with the onion. Remove from the heat and stir the vinegar through.

Serve warm, or at room temperature. The red pepper braise will keep in a lidded ceramic container in the fridge for 4–5 days.

My father used to grow zucchini in his backyard vegetable garden, and Mamma was always trying to find new ways to cook them, as the plants were so prolific. There was peperonata with zucchini (see page 92), grilled zucchini (see page 28) and stuffed zucchini. At the age of 87, she surprised us all with this rather delicious, buttery, zucchini dish, which she wrote down for me after we pronounced it was our new favourite way to eat zucchini. We had no idea where it emerged from, and it was only while writing this book that I found it in a Lisa Biondi cookbook (see page 141).

You need a kilo (just over 2 pounds) of zucchini for this recipe, so it's a great way to use up excess large overgrown zucchini. If your zucchini are overly large, I recommend scooping out the large seeds from the centre and trimming away the skin as well, which can be slightly bitter.

This dish is tasty and delicate and can be served as a side to grilled chicken, or even tossed through pasta.

Zucchini with prosciutto

ZUCCHINI CON PROSCIUTTO

SERVES 2-3 IN A PASTA SAUCE, OR 4-6 AS A SIDE DISH

1 kg (2 lb 3 oz) zucchini (courgettes)
70 g (2½ oz) unsalted butter
1 small white or brown onion, finely diced
125 ml (½ cup) dry white wine
50 g (1¾ oz) lean prosciutto, cut into small dice
handful of grated parmesan
chopped parsley, for sprinkling

Cut the zucchini into rounds about 1 cm (½ inch) thick. Cut each round into quarters and set aside.

Place 50 g (1¾ oz) of the butter in a large saucepan and melt over medium–low heat. Cook the onion for about 10 minutes, stirring occasionally, until softened and golden.

Add the zucchini and cook over medium–high heat for about 10 minutes, stirring fairly frequently so the zucchini doesn't burn.

Stir in the wine and season with salt and freshly cracked black pepper to taste. Cook for a couple of minutes, to allow some of the wine to evaporate, then reduce the heat. Cover and cook for about 20 minutes, until the zucchini is tender, stirring occasionally.

Add the remaining butter and turn the heat to high for a few minutes, to further caramelise the zucchini.

Stir in the prosciutto and parmesan and remove from the heat. Sprinkle with parsley and serve.

This is the only way my husband, Mark, eats brussels sprouts – the way he ate them at my mother's house for lunch. He was surprised how good they tasted, given his previous experiences with sad over-boiled ones.

Brussels sprouts with pancetta

CAVOLINI DI BRUXELLES TRIFOLATI

SERVES 4 AS A SIDE DISH

500 g (1 lb 2 oz) brussels
    sprouts
40 g (1½ oz) pancetta
2 teaspoons extra virgin olive
    oil, plus extra for drizzling
10 g (¼ oz) butter
1 garlic clove, finely diced
chopped parsley, for sprinkling

Wash the brussels sprouts well and cut in half through the stem. Bring a saucepan of salted water to the boil and drop in the sprout halves. Simmer for about 12 minutes, until tender, then drain.

Meanwhile, chop the pancetta into batons and place in a frying pan over medium–low heat with the olive oil and butter. Saute for about 10 minutes, by which time the pancetta should have softened and rendered much of its fat.

Add the garlic. After a minute or two, when the garlic is fragrant, drop in the brussels sprouts. Cover and cook for a further 10 minutes, or until the flavours have melded and the sprouts are cooked to your liking. Season with salt and freshly cracked black pepper to taste.

Serve warm as a side dish, with an extra drizzle of olive oil and scattered with parsley.

When I was a child, my father mysteriously grew mushrooms under the house. Much to my surprise, he would appear with a handful of them, seemingly out of nowhere, after he had gone downstairs to the cellar, and would re-emerge armed with said mushrooms and a bottle of wine. Braised mushrooms were hence a regular feature and favourite on the Bacchia table. Eventually he showed me how they grew in the warm darkness of the cellar; it is actually very easy to do at home with a kit from your local nursery!

I make this dish often, using a combination of Swiss brown and large flat mushrooms, adding dried porcini as well. They are delicious for breakfast on toast, added to an omelette, over polenta or in a mushroom risotto.

Braised mushrooms

FUNGHI TRIFOLATI

SERVES 3-4 AS A SIDE

10 g (¼ oz) dried porcini
    mushrooms
500 g (1 lb 2 oz) mixed
    mushrooms
2 tablespoons extra virgin
    olive oil
1 garlic clove, finely chopped
125 ml (½ cup) dry vermouth or
    white wine
chopped parsley or picked
    thyme sprigs, for sprinkling

Soak the dried porcini in 60 ml (¼ cup) of hot (not boiling) water for about 15 minutes. Drain the rehydrated mushrooms, reserving the soaking water, and straining off impurities if needed. Chop any very large mushrooms and set aside.

Wipe the fresh mushrooms clean with a tea towel. Cut into slices about 1 cm (½ inch) thick, and chop any larger mushroom slices in half.

Warm the olive oil in a large frying pan over medium heat. Add the garlic. After a minute or two, when fragrant, add the chopped fresh mushrooms. They will quickly soak up all the oil; gently stir them with a wooden spoon so they heat through evenly.

Pour in the vermouth and turn the heat up high. Allow the vermouth to evaporate; this will only take a couple of minutes. Pour in the reserved mushroom soaking water, along with the rehydrated porcini mushrooms, and reduce the heat to medium. By now the mushrooms should have softened and be starting to release their own juices.

Cover and simmer for about 15 minutes. Remove the lid and cook, uncovered, for a final 5 minutes, to allow the excess liquid to concentrate.

Season with salt and freshly cracked black pepper to taste. Scatter with herbs before serving.

When Mamma said she had made *peperonata*, it was usually followed by a chorus of 'which one'? She had many versions. The two common ingredients were red bell peppers - *peperoni* in Italian - and garlic. She made this version with zucchini, another version with eggplant (aubergine) and lots of tomato (see page 97), and still another with red onion and a splash of vinegar (see page 82). Sometimes she just put everything in. I rather suspect *peperonata* was a type of vegetable 'fridge clean' dish during summer - but always to a delicious result: simple vegetable side dishes for meats or fish on the grill. As a bonus, many of the recipes make a great base for a risotto, or pasta sauce.

Peperonata with zucchini & red pepper

PEPERONATA CON ZUCCHINI E PEPERONI

SERVES 4-6 AS A SIDE

3 tablespoons extra virgin
    olive oil
1 small brown onion, diced
1 garlic clove, finely chopped
3 zucchini (courgettes), about
    900 g (2 lb) in total, cut into
    1 cm (½ inch) rounds, then
    cut in half
1 red bell pepper (capsicum),
    finely sliced, then cut into
    bite-sized lengths
40 ml (1¼ fl oz) dry white wine
2 tablespoons tomato passata
    (pureed tomatoes)
1 bay leaf
handful of grated parmesan
    (optional)

Warm the olive oil in a large deep frying pan over medium–low heat. Add the onion with a good pinch of salt and cook for about 12 minutes, stirring frequently, until translucent, softened and golden. Add the garlic and cook for a few minutes, until fragrant.

Add the zucchini and red pepper. Once warmed through, turn up the heat and add the wine, and cook for a few minutes, until it mostly evaporates.

Reduce the heat to medium and stir in the passata. Add the bay leaf. When the mixture starts to bubble away, reduce the heat, cover and simmer for about 20 minutes, stirring occasionally. The zucchini should be releasing its liquid by now and starting to soften.

Remove the lid. Adjust the heat to keep the pan at a simmer, then cook, uncovered, for a further 15–20 minutes, until most of the liquid slowly evaporates. By now the zucchini should be starting to collapse. Season with salt to taste and give it a good stir.

Serve sprinkled with freshly cracked black pepper and grated parmesan, if desired.

FACTORY DAYS: HAM & CHEESE TOASTIES FOR LUNCH

For most of her working life in Australia, Mamma was a machinist: making socks at Holeproof, lingerie at Berlei and, eventually, canvas blinds at Campbell & Heeps. Lunch at the factory was, without fail, a toasted ham and cheese sandwich and a piece of fruit. She would make the sandwiches for both my father and herself after dinner the night before, using bread from a box loaf rather than the usual crusty bread rolls. Ever the practical person, sandwiches from a box loaf were easier to wrap and pack into a handbag. At home, she would toast the slices of bread, slice the ingredients, assemble the sandwich and cut it in half diagonally: one sandwich for her, and two for my father. There was never butter on the bread. She would then wrap them in foil. Having lived through World War II, she was accustomed to frugality and would use the same piece of foil day after day until it became tattered and had to be replaced by a fresh sheet. My father would dutifully bring home his sheets of foil each day as well.

In the morning, my parents left for work before 7 am, waking us girls before they departed. I would find the breakfast table set and a glass of freshly squeezed orange juice waiting on the table. My mother never learnt to drive – and in those days, no-one could afford to own and run two cars – so they went together, my father dropping her off at her workplace every morning, then driving a further 20 minutes to his own factory job.

When lunchtime came around, Mamma would retrieve the sandwich from her handbag and place it, foil wrapping and all, on top of the heater that was close to her feet under the sewing machine table. It was one of those bar heaters with a metal grill on top; each machinist had one by their feet, on the often cold and draughty factory floor. The heater warmed the already toasted sandwich through the foil on one side, only slightly melting the cheese, then Mamma would flip it over to warm the other side. She would then carefully lift it off the heater and open the foil to be greeted by a warming and satisfying toastie of sorts – warm toasted

> " When lunchtime came around, Mamma would retrieve the sandwich from her handbag and place it, foil wrapping and all, on top of the heater that was close to her feet under the sewing machine table.

bread filled with ham and melted cheese. She would fold the used foil and place it back in her bag, to be used for the next day's lunch.

In the late afternoon, my father would pick her up and they would drive back home. Papà was invariably so hungry after work that he would start seeing black spots – 'Gho così tanta fame che vedo scuro davanti i oci!', or so he proclaimed. Mamma would don an apron and start preparing dinner, mostly starting everything from scratch, as my father wasn't fond of leftovers. Her working day would end well into the evening, after she had hand-washed and dried all the dishes, and made the toasted sandwiches for their work lunch the next day. (Mamma had a dishwasher, but doubted its ability to wash the dishes to her satisfaction. She only ever used it when we had guests over, and even then she'd give the dishes a thorough rinse before loading them.) We children only occasionally helped her with dinner, as we had homework to do. And world affairs were of great importance to Papà, so after dinner he was busy with the newspaper and the television news. And she never ever complained.

In the past, eggplant was salted before using to remove bitterness - though most eggplants sold by greengrocers these days are not really bitter. That said, I still salt the diced eggplant for this recipe, as I find it is a great way of seasoning the dish. It does take some time, so feel free to omit this step.

This dish makes a main meal for vegetarians, a substantial side dish, and can also be used as a base for a couple of batches of pasta. It can also be halved and used in a risotto for four people (see recipe on page 62).

Peperonata with eggplant & tomato

PEPERONATA CON MELANZANE E POMODORI

SERVES 6-8 AS A SIDE

2 eggplants (aubergines), about 900 g (2 lb) in total
1 tablespoon salt, for salting the eggplant
3 tablespoons extra virgin olive oil
1 small white onion, diced
1 garlic clove, finely diced
1–2 red bell peppers (capsicums), cut into 2–3 cm (¾–1¼ inch) dice
440 g (15½ oz) tinned peeled tomatoes
2–3 basil stalks

Cut the eggplant into 3–4 cm (1¼–1½ inch) chunks. Place in a large bowl and toss with the salt, rubbing it into the eggplant pieces with your fingertips. Set aside on a wire rack to drain for about 45 minutes. Rinse under running water and pat dry.

Warm the olive oil in a large frying pan over medium–low heat. Saute the onion with a good pinch of salt for about 10 minutes. Add the garlic. After a minute or two, when fragrant, add the eggplant and bell pepper to heat through.

Add the tomatoes, breaking any larger ones into smaller pieces with a wooden spoon. Rinse the tomato tin with a few tablespoons of water and add that to the frying pan as well, along with the basil stalks.

Once everything is bubbling away, reduce the heat and put the lid on. Simmer for about 45 minutes, adding a splash more water if needed, or until the eggplant is cooked through but not totally collapsed. Taste for salt, especially if you omitted salting the eggplant pieces earlier; if you did salt the eggplant, you may not need any extra salt.

Remove the basil stalks and serve warm. Any leftovers will keep in a ceramic or glass lidded container in the fridge for up to 1 week.

Younger greens are delicious in this recipe, having tender leaves and thin stems that do not require trimming. In Italy, these are readily available, though elsewhere they can be harder to find, unless you grow your own. When buying from a greengrocer, I use regular silverbeet as the leafy green of choice, and trim away most of the thick stem (which you can reserve for another use, such as the vegetable soup on page 36).

You will find this recipe, or a similar one, all along the coast of Istria and down through Dalmatia. It is a perfect accompaniment to grilled meats or seafood; we also loved it topped with a simple tomato sugo.

Potatoes & silverbeet

PATATE CON LE ERBETTE

SERVES 4

650 g (1 lb 7 oz) all-purpose potatoes
1 bunch of silverbeet (Swiss chard)
3 tablespoons extra virgin olive oil
1 garlic clove, finely chopped

Peel the potatoes and chop into 6–8 pieces, depending on their size. Remove the thick spines from the silverbeet. Wash the leaves well, then chop into smallish pieces. Set aside.

Place the potatoes in a large saucepan filled with salted water. Bring to the boil, then cook for 10–15 minutes, until the potato is cooked through and just starting to fall apart when prodded with a fork. For the last 2–3 minutes, add the silverbeet. Drain, reserving about 125 ml (½ cup) of the cooking water.

Wash and dry the pan. Warm the olive oil and garlic over medium heat. After a minute or two, when fragrant, add the cooked potato and silverbeet, stirring to infuse them with the garlic and olive oil.

Mash the potatoes gently with a fork, then add a bit of the cooking water to obtain the desired consistency. Once warmed through, season to taste with salt.

So simple, hearty and colourful, this dish was a favourite of Mamma's in her late 80s. It is fabulous in a risotto, to make a kind of *risi e bisi e salsiccia* ('rice, peas and sausage') – a spin on the risi e bisi (see page 61) from the Veneto that Mamma knew so well and loved. This braise can be served as part of a main meal for two with a side of potatoes and salad, or in a hearty risotto for two (see page 62 for the risotto method), or as a pasta sauce to serve two or three.

Peas & sausages

PISELLI E SALSICCIA

SERVES 2 AS A MAIN

250 g (9 oz) frozen peas
2 good-quality pork and fennel
    sausages
1 tablespoon extra virgin
    olive oil
60 ml (¼ cup) dry white wine
60 ml (¼ cup) warm beef stock
    or chicken stock, or hot
    water
chopped parsley, for sprinkling

Remove the peas from the freezer and leave in a bowl on the benchtop.

Chop each sausage into bite-sized chunks. You can remove the casings if you like, though I usually don't. Place in a frying pan with the olive oil over medium heat. Allow to brown all over, turning as needed.

Increase the heat to medium–high and pour in the wine. Allow that to mostly evaporate, then reduce the heat to medium and add the peas, which will have partially thawed. Pour in the stock and bring to a simmer.

Cover the pan, reduce the heat and allow to bubble away for about 15 minutes, until the sausages are cooked through. There shouldn't be much residual liquid; if there is, allow to cook, uncovered, until it evaporates. Season with salt and freshly cracked black pepper to taste and remove from the heat.

Scatter with parsley and serve.

Admiring the vegetable garden, Vermont South, Melbourne (1985).

If we didn't have pasta, rice or polenta as part of a meal, we would have potatoes; a meal just wasn't complete without one of these. This is the simplest of dishes, but so delicious and quick to make. Mamma would call it *calandraca*, though if you look up the word, you will find the dish includes meat – so she would add the words *senza carne* ('meatless').

This is a great dish to serve with steak or schnitzel, or even on its own when you are having a simple lunch for one. It is like a warm hug.

Potato & tomato stew

CALANDRACA (SENZA CARNE)

SERVES 4 AS A HEARTY SIDE

750 g (1 lb 11 oz) all-purpose
     potatoes, such as desiree
2 tablespoons extra virgin
     olive oil
1 garlic clove, finely chopped
400 g (14 oz) tin peeled and
     chopped tomatoes
a good pinch of dried oregano
     (see Note)

Peel the potatoes and cut into four or six pieces, depending on their size.

Warm the olive oil in a saucepan over medium heat with the garlic. After a minute or two, when the garlic becomes fragrant, add the tomatoes. Half-fill the tomato tin with water, swirl it around to collect any remaining tomato, then add the water to the pan, stirring well.

Once the sauce warms through, season with a good amount of salt. Gently drop in the potatoes, stirring to coat them well in the sauce.

Once the pan starts bubbling away, reduce the heat to a simmer. Stir in the oregano. Cover and simmer for about 20 minutes, or until the potatoes are fork-tender and starting to fall apart. Taste and adjust for salt.

NOTE: You can use dried basil instead of oregano, if you like, and also a good pinch of chilli flakes.

Mamma used to cook her stuffed tomatoes at the same time and with the same stuffing as her stuffed green bell peppers (capsicums), the shell of the tomatoes collapsing faster than the peppers. She would use grosse lisse tomatoes that my father had grown in the garden, placing them all quite tightly in her orange electric frying pan.

Large heirloom tomatoes will yield the tastiest result with this simple dish. How much space there is within the tomatoes for the stuffing depends on the tomato variety and their size, so you are better off buying more tomatoes than you might need, and save any spares for other uses.

Mamma didn't put potatoes in the pan with the tomatoes, but I have found they soak up the lovely juices that are released during baking – and potatoes cooked this way are just delicious!

Stuffed tomatoes

POMODORI RIPIENI

MAKES 8-10

8–10 large tomatoes
120 g (4½ oz) medium-grain white rice
60 ml (¼ cup) extra virgin olive oil, plus extra for drizzling
1 small brown or white onion, finely diced
2 garlic cloves, finely diced
400 g (14 oz) minced (ground) beef
75 g (2¾ oz) pitted green or black olives, chopped
½ teaspoon freshly grated nutmeg
½ teaspoon Hungarian paprika
60 g (2 oz) parmesan, grated
large handful of parsley leaves
3 large all-purpose potatoes, peeled and cut into smallish wedges

Slice the tops off your tomatoes using a sharp knife. Set the tomato tops aside as lids for your stuffed tomatoes. Using a paring knife and a spoon, carefully remove the tomato seeds and some of the core, keeping some of the internal structure intact, so the tomatoes retain their shape after stuffing. Separate the seeds from the tomato flesh. Finely chop the tomato flesh and reserve with any juices. Place the tomato shells upside down to drain.

Rinse the rice under cold running water. Bring a small saucepan of water to the boil and drop in the rice. Bring back to the boil and parboil the rice for 5 minutes. Drain and set aside.

Warm half the olive oil in a large frying pan over medium–low heat. Toss in the onion and saute with a good pinch of salt for about 12 minutes, stirring occasionally, until translucent and becoming golden. Next, add the garlic and saute for a minute or two, until fragrant.

Add the beef and increase the heat to medium–high. Cook the meat for a few minutes, stirring frequently so it browns evenly all over. Turn the heat to low and add the reserved tomato flesh and juices. After a few minutes, add the parboiled rice, olives, spices and a good pinch of salt. Stir until well combined and cook for a few more minutes; the mixture will be only slightly saucy.

Remove from the heat and stir the parmesan and parsley through. Set aside to cool slightly.

Preheat the oven to 160°C (320°F) fan-forced. Select a baking dish large enough to fit all the tomatoes and potatoes. Swirl the remaining olive oil around the base of the dish. Add the potato wedges and massage them with the oil, using a little extra oil if needed. Season with salt.

Drizzle a tiny bit of olive oil inside each tomato and scatter with a bit of salt. Spoon the filling into the tomatoes and top with the 'lids'. Carefully arrange the stuffed tomatoes in the baking dish, nestling them among the potato. Drizzle more olive oil over the lot, then cover with foil.

Bake for 45 minutes, then remove the foil and bake for a further 45 minutes. The potato should be golden and cooked through, and the tomatoes nicely browned – don't worry if the tomatoes have collapsed or split slightly. Enjoy warm, or at room temperature.

Opposite: Livia, Paola and Barbara, Box Hill South, Melbourne (1965).
This page: Livia's home in via Fossabiuba, Mansuè, Veneto (2022).

Thin French-style crepes were called *palacinche* at home, a reflection of my father's Istrian origins. They were also called omlet or crepe (always singular), never the Italian *crespelle*. When stuffed, rolled and shaped into cigars, we called them *cannelloni*. Growing up, my mother would stuff the crepes with ricotta, spinach and chicken, but I love the simplicity of the spinach and silverbeet version below.

This dish is great for a dinner party as you can make the crepes the day before, stack them and pop them in the fridge, then take them out of the fridge an hour before assembling.

Crepes with spinach & fontina

CREPE AL FORNO CON SPINACI E FONTINA

SERVES 4-6

3 eggs
500 ml (2 cups) milk
225 g (1½ cups) plain
    (all-purpose) flour
15-25 g (½-1 oz) unsalted butter

For the filling
1 large bunch of English spinach
5-6 large silverbeet (Swiss
    chard) stalks
1 tablespoon extra virgin
    olive oil
1 garlic clove, finely diced
60 g (2 oz) parmesan, grated,
    plus extra to serve
1 egg, lightly beaten
½ teaspoon freshly grated
    nutmeg
70 g (2½ oz) fontina (or other
    favourite melting cheese),
    cut into thin batons
50 g (1¾ oz) unsalted butter

To make the crepes, whisk the eggs and milk in a large jug and set aside. Place the flour and a good pinch of salt in a large bowl. Pour in about half the liquid, whisking as you go, then pour in the remaining liquid and whisk until smooth. Set aside for 30 minutes in a cool spot.

Place a 21-23 cm (8¼-9 inch) non-stick frying pan over medium heat. Add a teaspoon of the butter and swirl it around the pan. Add a generous 60 ml (¼ cup) of batter to the pan, swirling it quickly so it evenly coats the surface, with just a small space at the edge so you can easily flip it over. It should take about a minute to turn golden, and for the edges to lift slightly. Flip over onto the other side using a spatula and cook until golden. Lift onto a plate and repeat with the remaining batter. Add a bit more butter when needed, although you won't need a lot if the pan is non-stick. You should end up with 9-10 crepes. Stack the crepes on top of each other until ready to use.

To make the filling, wash the spinach and silverbeet leaves in plenty of water. Remove any damaged leaves and stalks. Remove the thick stalks from the silverbeet and roughly chop the leaves.

Bring a large saucepan of salted water to the boil. Drop in the chopped silverbeet leaves and boil for a few minutes, then add the spinach leaves and cook for a few more minutes. Remove from the heat and drain. When cool, finely chop and set aside.

Warm the olive oil and garlic in large frying pan over medium heat. Add the blanched greens and saute for a few minutes, until infused with the garlic. Transfer to a bowl and set aside to cool. Add the parmesan, egg and nutmeg and season with salt and freshly cracked black pepper, mixing well.

Preheat the oven to 160°C (320°F) fan-forced.

Select a large baking dish that will fit all the rolled-up crepes in a single layer. Smear some of the butter over the base. Place a few tablespoons of filling on one edge of a crepe and top with a few batons of fontina. Roll the crepe up to form a cigar and place in the baking dish. Repeat with the remaining crepes and filling.

Melt the remaining butter and brush over the rolled-up crepes. Bake for 12 minutes, or until the crepes are warmed through and the cheese has melted.

Serve immediately, scattered with extra parmesan.

Opposite: Motta di Livenza, Veneto (2022).
This page: Out to dinner in Melbourne (1954).

FISH & MEAT

1. Prawn & scallop skewers
2. Fish fillets with onion, anchovies & capers
3. Salmon baked with salsa verde
4. Oven-roasted chicken thighs with mustard & leeks
5. Celebration roast chicken
6. Pizza-style escalopes
7. Schnitzels with ham, cheese & artichoke
8. Little meatballs in tomato sugo
9. Italian meatloaf with eggs
10. Clara's slow-cooked beef stew

Christmas in Australia falls in summer. Though many follow the European tradition of roasted hams or poultry, here it is common to have seafood on the table. If we decided on a seafood-based Christmas lunch, Papà would see Steve the fishmonger and buy several kilos each of prawns and scallops. He took great pride in a rare contribution to cooking: barbecuing dozens of skewers of prawns and scallops. My mother made the marinade and threaded the skewers, and after an hour or two, the skewers would be barbecued on the back terrace, creating a plume of smoke and the most delicious smell. My father would proudly bring them indoors to the grandchildren, who adored them, easily devouring three or more skewers each.

This recipe can be easily doubled, tripled or quadrupled to feed more. The inclusion of orange zest in the marinade adds a lovely brightness to the seafood skewers, which are wonderful with a side of potatoes and salad.

Prawn & scallop skewers

SPIEDINI DI GAMBERI E CAPESANTE

SERVES 2–3;
MAKES 6 SKEWERS

250 g (9 oz) raw prawns (shrimp), peeled and deveined, tails on, heads removed

250 g (9 oz) raw scallops, preferably with the roe attached

60 ml (¼ cup) extra virgin olive oil, plus extra for brushing

1 garlic clove, crushed

zest of 1 small lemon

zest of 1 small orange

1 tablespoon chopped parsley, plus extra for sprinkling

lemon wedges, to serve

Wash the seafood and pat dry, then place in a lidded container.

Place the olive oil, garlic, lemon zest, orange zest and parsley in a small bowl and stir to combine. Pour the marinade over the seafood, massaging it into the prawns and scallops with your fingertips. Cover and marinate in the fridge for at least 1 hour, but no more than 2–3 hours.

If using bamboo skewers, soak them in water for 15 minutes before using, so they don't scorch during cooking.

About 15 minutes before cooking, remove the seafood from the fridge to bring it to room temperature. Thread the prawns and scallops onto separate skewers (as they have different cooking times), being careful not to crowd them on the skewers.

Heat a barbecue or chargrill pan to medium–high. Cook the prawn skewers first, by brushing one side with olive oil and placing that side down on the hotplate or pan. After about 2 minutes, carefully flip them over using tongs, then cook for another few minutes until they turn a nicely striped orange. Transfer to a warmed plate.

Cook the scallop skewers in the same way, but reduce the cooking time to about 1 minute on each side. You don't want to overcook scallops as they can turn rubbery. Serve warm, with lemon wedges, and scattered with extra parsley.

Mamma and I would make this dish together when she was living on her own. It's salty, sour and a little sweet, and reminded her of the quintessential Venetian dish, *bigoli in salsa*. This recipe is an amalgam of a couple of Marcella Hazan recipes with a few of Mamma's suggestions thrown in. I use whatever firm white fish I can find at a good price from the fishmonger – often flathead tails, but also sustainably caught swordfish or flake.

This dish works really well with a side of potatoes or fresh bread, to mop up the delicious sauce.

Fish fillets with onion, anchovies & capers

FILETTI DI PESCE CON CIPOLLA, ACCIUGHE E CAPPERI

SERVES 4

50 g (1¾ oz) salted capers
60 ml (¼ cup) extra virgin
    olive oil
2 brown or white onions, finely
    sliced into half-rings
6 anchovy fillets, chopped
1 garlic clove, finely chopped
800 g (1 lb 12 oz) firm-fleshed
    skinless white fish fillets
plain (all-purpose) flour, for
    dusting
60 ml (¼ cup) dry white wine
2 generous tablespoons white
    wine vinegar
handful of chopped parsley,
    for sprinkling

Place the capers in a small bowl, cover with water and set aside for at least 10 minutes to remove the excess salt.

In a lidded frying pan large enough to fit all the fish in a single layer, warm half the olive oil over medium–low heat. Add the onion and anchovies and saute for 10–12 minutes, stirring occasionally, until the onion is translucent and soft, but not yet golden. The anchovies should have completely dissolved. Add the garlic. After a few minutes, add the drained capers and stir them through. Transfer the mixture to a small bowl; it's fine if some of the oil remains in the pan.

Cut the fish fillets to whatever size you prefer – from steaks to bite-sized chunks. Dust with flour and sprinkle on some salt.

Warm the remaining olive oil in the pan over medium heat. Slip in the fish pieces. Cook on one side for a few minutes, until you see the flesh starting to turn white within the flaky chunks. How long this takes depends on the size and type of fish – let the colour be your guide. Carefully flip the fish over using a spatula, then cook the second side for a minute or two.

Turn the heat up a notch and add the wine. Let the wine partially evaporate, then add the sauteed onion mixture. Check the fish pieces haven't stuck to the base of the pan by carefully lifting them up with the spatula. Pour in the vinegar, put the lid on, then reduce the heat so the sauce is simmering. Leave to simmer for about 5 minutes, or until the fish is cooked through and the flavours have melded.

Remove from the heat, taste for salt and scatter with the parsley just before serving.

Nello and Livia announcing the impending
arrival of their first child, Melbourne (1954).

In the 1990s, when both my parents had retired, they spent a lot of time trying new recipes. When I say they 'tried' new recipes, my mother cooked, and my father ate. He occasionally tested flavours and combinations through the preparation, but his involvement was minimal – and once salmon fillets were introduced into her repertoire, they never left. This recipe was a family favourite, though often my mother omitted the dill, as it wasn't growing in the garden, and simply upped the quantity of parsley, which we always had in abundance. I rather like the dill, as it goes so well with salmon.

Salmon baked with salsa verde

SALMONE CON SALSA VERDE

SERVES 4

fine sea salt, for sprinkling
4 × 200 g (7 oz) skinless
    salmon fillets, pin bones
    removed
chopped dill, for sprinkling
chopped parsley, for sprinkling
lemon wedges, to serve

Salsa verde
2 tablespoons salted capers
handful of parsley leaves
1 heaped tablespoon dill fronds
1 garlic clove, roughly chopped
3 anchovy fillets
1 heaped tablespoon pine nuts
2 teaspoons French or dijon
    mustard
70 ml (2¼ fl oz) extra virgin
    olive oil
20 ml (¾ fl oz) freshly squeezed
    lemon juice

Preheat the oven to 180°C (350°F) fan-forced. Line a baking tray with baking paper.

To make the salsa verde, place the capers in a small bowl, cover with water and set aside for at least 10 minutes to remove the excess salt.

Place the parsley, dill, garlic, anchovies, pine nuts and mustard in a food processor. Drain the capers and add those as well, then pulse until homogenous. Add the olive oil and lemon juice and process until combined. The salsa verde should be easily spreadable; add a splash more lemon juice if needed.

Sprinkle some fine sea salt on one side of each salmon fillet. Place the salmon portions on the baking tray, salted side down. Using a teaspoon, spread the salsa verde over the top, reserving a little for serving. Bake for 10 minutes.

Rest the salmon for a few minutes out of the oven. Scatter with parsley and dill and serve with a lemon wedge and the remaining salsa verde on the side.

MENU PLANNING

My mother's careful planning of food and menus for the week was born of necessity. In the 1970s and 1980s, every Thursday evening she would write a shopping list for the weekend and week ahead. She never learnt to drive, and food shopping was done once a week on a Friday afternoon by my father. Back then, shops were open late one night per week, and closed at noon on a Saturday. There was no Sunday trading. Last-minute shopping for recipe ingredients was not possible, except at the local milk bar, where the shelves were mostly bare.

Impromptu meals, even if guests dropped by, were dictated entirely by what was in the house. That is where her preserves came in handy; it was easy to whip up some roasted tomato pesto for a plate of pasta and serve apricot jam crostata or almond crescents with coffee. And because Mamma always made enough for several meals, there was often a leftover vegetable braise or meat ragù that could easily be turned into a risotto. She was very good at looking in the pantry or fridge and swiftly working out what she could make with what she had available. And every meal was accompanied by a green salad – sometimes just the green leafy radicchio that Papà grew in the garden.

Menu planning with the recipes in this book, my Mamma's recipes, brings me great pleasure. It takes me back to her kitchen, to her chatter, her laughter and her patience when she was teaching me how to prepare a dish. And, of course, the joy of eating her food.

A simple family lunch
Schnitzels with ham, cheese & artichoke (page 134)
Potato salad with basil pesto (page 74)
A side of green beans & tomatoes (page 78)
Isa's pear cake (page 178)

Al fresco summer meal
Grilled vegetable platter (page 28)
Focaccia with milk (page 44)
Prawn & scallop skewers (page 116)
Amaretti & chocolate semifreddo (page 195)

Winter lunch for two
Rich chicken egg-drop soup (page 34)
Braised mushrooms as a risotto (page 90)
A side of brussels sprouts with pancetta (page 89)
Buttery almond crescents with coffee (page 157)

For when guests drop by unexpectedly
Spaghetti with oven-roasted tomato pesto (page 48)
Peas & sausages (page 100)
Apricot jam crostata (page 162)

Tamara's birthday lunch (gluten free)
Asparagus gratin with walnuts (page 18)
Rice, peas & prosciutto (page 61)
Italian meatloaf with eggs (page 142)
A side of potatoes & silverbeet (page 98)
Vanilla panna cotta with strawberries (page 170)

Anniversary dinner
Figs with prosciutto & blue cheese (page 16)
Cannelloni with ricotta, spinach & oven-roasted
    tomatoes (page 56)
Salmon baked with salsa verde (page 122)
Hazelnut & chocolate layer cake (page 185)

We always had dijon mustard in the fridge, mainly to eat with boiled meats, pork sausages or ham. Mamma also paired it with chicken, garlic and wine in a dish she cooked in the electric frying pan. I used to think there was cream in this dish, as the sauce that was spooned over the chicken was so creamy. The leeks are my addition, and make an ideal bed for the chicken thighs as they braise in the pan juices. This dish is lovely with mashed or pan-cooked potatoes, polenta or even bread – anything that will catch the lovely sauce.

Oven-roasted chicken thighs with mustard & leeks

POLLO CON SENAPE E PORRI

SERVES 6

2 large leeks
6 chicken thighs, skin on and bone in
2 tablespoons extra virgin olive oil
80 ml (⅓ cup) white wine or dry white vermouth
1 garlic clove, finely chopped
15 g (½ oz) butter
2 heaped tablespoons dijon mustard
1 teaspoon dried thyme
200 ml (7 fl oz) good-quality chicken stock
a squeeze of lemon juice

Preheat the oven to 160°C (320°F) fan-forced.

Finely slice the white and pale green stem of the leeks, discarding the roots and tough darker green leaves. Soak the leek slices in a large bowl of water, massaging them briefly with your fingers to dislodge any dirt stuck in the layers. Drain and set aside.

Wash the chicken thighs and pat dry with paper towel. Scatter on salt and freshly cracked black pepper.

In a frying pan large enough to fit all the chicken in a single layer, warm the olive oil over medium–high heat. Place the chicken in the pan, skin side down. Fry for about 5 minutes, until the skin is golden. Carefully flip the chicken over and fry the other side for about 4 minutes, until it browns. Increase the heat, pour in the wine and allow to partially evaporate for a few minutes. Leaving the juices in the pan, lift out the chicken pieces and transfer to a large baking dish.

Reduce the stovetop heat to medium. Add the leek slices, garlic and butter to the pan. Stir in the mustard and thyme, then pour in the stock and season with salt and pepper. Braise the leek, uncovered, for about 15 minutes, stirring now and then.

Pour the saucy leeks over and around the chicken. Cover with a lid or foil. Transfer to the oven and bake for 45 minutes.

Remove the lid or foil and bake for a further 20 minutes, or until the chicken is nicely roasted and cooked through.

Allow to rest for a few minutes before serving with a squeeze of lemon.

This very special chicken dish was made for celebrations, usually Easter Sunday or a special birthday. Its heightened specialness is due to the amazing feat of Mamma removing the chicken carcass whole, stuffing the chicken with a savoury bomb of a filling and sewing the whole lot back up again. Friends would come over to watch her perform this act, taking notes as she did it. Her knives were not sharp – but clearly her knowledge of chicken anatomy was! The family would wistfully remember Nonna's special chicken and talk about it so often that I decided to learn how to prepare it. Armed with a sharp, flexible knife and a few clips on YouTube, I managed to do what no one else in the family had yet tried, and so the baton (or rather knife, needle and thread) have now been passed on to me. I wonder which of the grandchildren or great-grandchildren will eventually take up the challenge?

If the process of deboning a chicken seems complex, a speciality butcher may be able to do it for you. This recipe is based on the one in Lisa Biondi's book (see page 141) on meats.

Celebration roast chicken

POLLO RIPIENO ARROSTO

SERVES 8-10

1.8 kg (4 lb) chicken
80 g (2¾ oz) ham, cut in
    a single slice
80 g (2¾ oz) pressed tongue,
    cut in a single slice (or use
    80 g/2¾ oz extra ham)
50 g (1¾ oz) butter, melted
100 ml (3½ fl oz) brandy

For the filling

200 g (7 oz) minced (ground)
    veal or beef
100 g (3½ oz) minced (ground)
    pork
100 g (3½ oz) pork sausage,
    casings removed
2 small eggs

Preheat the oven to 170°C (340°F) fan-forced.

To prepare the chicken, lay it front side down, with the neck closest to you. Cut the skin along the spine from the neck through to the tail, keeping a portion of the skin at the neck connected. Using a very sharp knife (one with a flexible blade if possible) and one of the free online YouTube clips to help you, carefully separate the carcass from the chicken, one side at a time, keeping the wings and drumsticks in situ. Use the carcass to make broth (see page 34).

Wash the chicken and pat dry. Lay it out flat on your work surface, skin side down, with the tail end of the chicken closest to you.

Combine the filling ingredients in a bowl. Season with salt and freshly cracked black pepper and mix well to make a compact filling mixture. Cut the ham and tongue slices into four or five batons.

Lightly salt the chicken. Spread half the filling onto the chicken. Arrange half the meat batons on top, alternating ham and tongue. Cover with the remaining filling, then the remaining alternating meat batons. Bring the sides of the chicken to the centre (it is easier if someone helps you). Carefully sew the chicken together along its back, up to the neck opening.

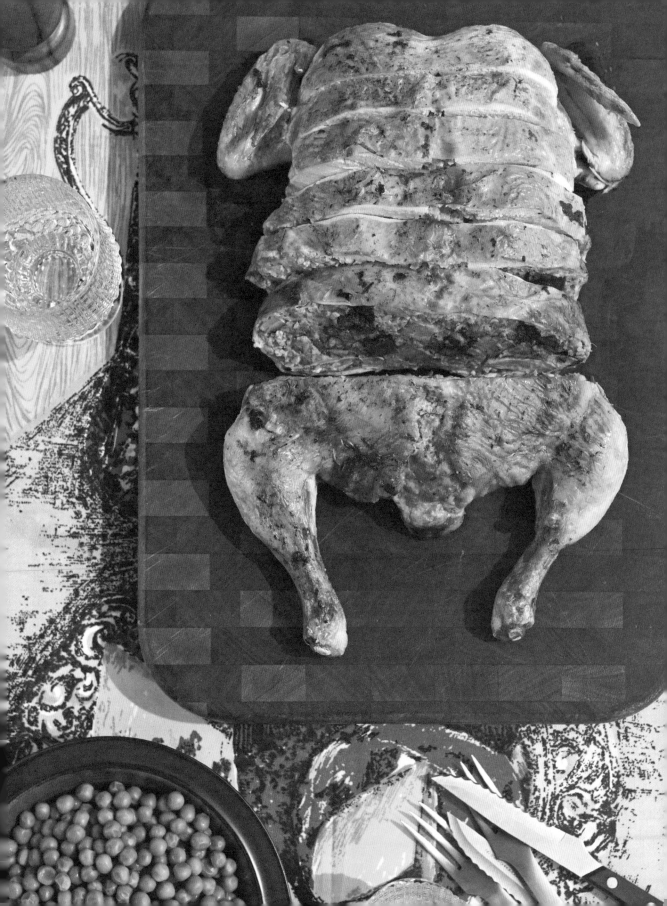

50 g (½ cup) grated parmesan
1 tablespoon finely chopped
    parsley
1 slice (30 g/1 oz) crustless
    bread, soaked in milk,
    squeezed
20 g (¾ oz) shelled pistachios,
    left whole
½ teaspoon freshly grated
    nutmeg

Pour the melted butter into a large roasting tin. Lay the chicken in the tin, seam side down. Roast for about 15 minutes, or until turning golden.

Gently heat the brandy in a small saucepan (don't let it boil). Pour the brandy over the chicken and roast for at least another 1½ hours, basting occasionally with the pan juices. The chicken is cooked when the skin is deeply golden, and the internal temperature reaches a steady 75°C (167°F) when tested with a meat thermometer.

Remove from the oven and allow to rest for at least 20 minutes before slicing. Strain the juices in the pan and use as a sauce for the chicken slices.

The chicken is also lovely at room temperature.

Opposite: Paola and Livia on the bonnet of the Holden
station wagon, Neerim South, Melbourne (1967).

This page: Oderzo, Veneto (2022).

My father was a carnivore, as well as a lover of fish, pasta, vegetables ... and he had a sweet tooth. He loved pretty much all food – but would scoff if we served him anything with a whiff of coriander or cinnamon. This classic 1970s dish was a firm family favourite and satisfied my father's love of meat on a weeknight. It was so fast to make. And so easy. And so good. Make sure the meat is very thin by beating it with a meat mallet between two sheets of baking paper, or ask your butcher to pound the meat for you to ensure the slices cook quickly.

These escalopes are wonderful served with fresh bread or mashed potatoes, to mop up all the tasty sauce. And a green side salad doesn't go astray, either.

Pizza-style escalopes

BISTECCHE ALLA PIZZAIOLA

SERVES 4

4 thin yearling beef steaks, about 5 mm (¼ inch) thick, and weighing about 180 g (6½ oz) each
40 ml (1¼ fl oz) extra virgin olive oil
15 g (½ oz) unsalted butter
1 garlic clove, crushed
400 g (14 oz) tin peeled tomatoes, roughly chopped and drained
a generous pinch of dried oregano

About an hour before cooking, take the meat out of the fridge to bring it to room temperature. Season with salt on both sides and allow to rest while you get everything else ready.

Place the olive oil and butter in a large frying pan and turn the heat up high. Once the butter has melted, swirl together the butter and oil. Add the steaks (in batches if needed) and sear for a minute on each side. Leaving the juices in the pan, transfer the steaks to a warmed plate, cover with foil and set aside.

Reduce the stovetop heat to medium–low. Add the garlic to the pan and cook for a minute or two, until fragrant. Add the tomatoes and oregano. Cook for about 10 minutes, or until the sauce has thickened. Season with salt and freshly cracked black pepper to taste.

Slip the steaks (plus the juices that have accumulated on the plate) into the sauce, turning them over so the sauce clings to them. Allow to simmer for several minutes, until they are warmed through and cooked to your liking, and the sauce has thickened a bit more.

Serve immediately, on a warmed platter or on warmed plates.

Growing up, we ate veal schnitzel often, and on special occasions it was stuffed before being crumbed and pan-fried. The inspiration for this version of the filling is based on Lisa Biondi's recipe for *portafogli delizia* ('wallet delight'). The 'wallet' contains a filling of cheese, ham and thinly sliced artichoke. Yes, an absolute delight!

If you cannot find veal, or prefer not to use it, use pork or yearling beef.

Schnitzels with ham, cheese & artichoke

FILETTI AL PORTAFOGLIO IMPANATI

SERVES 4 GENEROUSLY

8 thin slices of veal, 700–750 g
    (1 lb 9 oz–1 lb 11 oz) in total
140 g (5 oz) shaved ham
140 g (5 oz) Emmental or
    fontina, thinly sliced
140 g (5 oz) marinated artichoke
    hearts, finely chopped
extra virgin olive oil, for
    pan-frying

For crumbing
1 large or 2 small eggs
1–2 tablespoons milk
plain (all-purpose) flour,
    for dusting
50/50 mix of dried
    breadcrumbs and
    Panko breadcrumbs

Place the veal slices between two sheets of baking paper on the bench and bang them with a meat mallet or rolling pin until they are about 5 mm (¼ inch) thick, even in thickness and measure about 13 cm × 9 cm (5 inches × 3½ inches). Some will be smaller or larger, but try to match them up so the slices are the same size.

Lightly salt the veal slices. Place the ham slices on top of four of the veal slices, to cover most of the meat, but leaving the edges free. Layer the cheese on top, then the artichokes. Top each with another veal slice of about the same size and press down to flatten.

In a large shallow bowl, lightly whisk the egg and milk using a fork. Spread some flour on a large plate, and the mixed breadcrumbs on another large plate.

You will need to crumb the double-layered schnitzel carefully. Place one schnitzel onto the plate of flour; pat lightly, then carefully sprinkle a layer of flour on top and pat lightly again. Lift the schnitzel out (I use my hands) and carefully turn it over, not allowing the two slices of veal to separate. Place the schnitzel in the egg and milk mixture to coat, then transfer to the plate of breadcrumbs; pat lightly, then carefully sprinkle a layer of breadcrumbs on top and pat them down. Place the schnitzel on a clean plate and repeat with the remaining schnitzels.

Warm a good amount of olive oil in a large frying pan over medium heat. Slip in the schnitzels, in batches if needed, and fry for about 4 minutes on each side, until the crumbs are golden, the cheese has melted and the meat is cooked through. Drain on paper towel.

Serve warm, with spinach or mashed potatoes.

The term 'meatballs' is a bit of a misnomer for the ones Mamma made; they were full of so much more than meat and were an absolute flavour bomb. They remained moist and delicious, whether cooked in the *fersora* (frying pan) as my mother did, and then dropped into the sauce, or simply cooked in the sauce – which is what I do (less washing up that way!).

I like to serve the polpettine on soft polenta, made with a good handful of grated parmesan and an equal amount of butter added once the polenta has cooked.

Little meatballs in tomato sugo

POLPETTINE CON SUGO

SERVES 4

2 tablespoons extra virgin
    olive oil
½ small onion, finely chopped
500 ml (2 cups) tomato passata
    (pureed tomatoes)
200 g (7 oz) tinned peeled
    tomatoes
2 basil stalks

For the meatballs
½ zucchini (courgette), grated
1 slice fresh bread
60 ml (¼ cup) milk
300 g (10½ oz) minced (ground)
    beef (or half beef, half pork)
½ small onion, coarsely grated
1 garlic clove, finely chopped
¼ teaspoon chilli flakes
½ small carrot, grated
6 large pitted black or green
    olives, finely chopped
40 g (1½ oz) grated parmesan
10–15 basil leaves, chopped
1 large egg, lightly beaten
40 g (1½ oz) dried breadcrumbs

Warm the olive oil in a large deep frying pan that will fit all the meatballs in a single layer. Add the onion and a pinch of salt and saute over medium–low heat for about 15 minutes, until the onion is translucent. Stir in the passata, tomatoes, basil stalks and 125 ml (½ cup) of water. Season with salt to taste. Allow to simmer slowly while you prepare the meatballs.

Place the zucchini in a small bowl and sprinkle with ¼ teaspoon of salt. Mix to combine, then squeeze the zucchini to remove the excess liquid. Transfer to a large bowl.

Remove the crusts from the bread, then soak the bread briefly in the milk and, again, squeeze out the excess liquid. Transfer the bread to the bowl with the zucchini and add the remaining meatball ingredients, along with a heaped ¼ teaspoon of salt.

Mix well, using a spoon initially, and then your hands, until well combined. Using wet hands, make walnut-sized balls, about 20 g (¾ oz) in weight, and lower them gently into the simmering sauce. Keep making more meatballs and dropping them in, giving the sauce a gentle stir to make sure the meatballs cook evenly.

After you drop the last meatball into the sauce, simmer for another 15 minutes or so. Taste for salt, remove the basil stalks and serve on a bed of soft polenta.

Top right: Albury, Australia (1950).

Opposite: Christmas at Alba and Fide's house,
Box Hill South, Melbourne (1976).

This page: The day before moving to Italy,
Box Hill South, Melbourne (1972).

MAMMA & HER COOKBOOKS

My mother was a very good cook who was often told that she should open her own restaurant. She would laugh it off and accept the compliment graciously, telling everyone that she had learnt to cook in Australia – from other Italian home cooks, and from two cookbooks: *Il Tesoretto della Cucina Italiana* (1947) by Giuseppe Oberosler, and a series of six hardcover books called *I Documentari di Lisa Biondi* (1969–1970).

The first of these, *Il Tesoretto*, is an old-fashioned, well-worn paperback with more than 1700 recipes and several diagrams. My uncle Fidenzio brought it out from Italy in 1952 and it informed my mother's cooking for the next 20 years. Ingredients are slotted in the cooking method, rather than being listed separately, and by today's standards quite a challenge to follow. There is a useful chapter on how to use leftovers in the kitchen, turning them into totally new meals, and a short but informative chapter on preserves. My favourite is the section on menus, with suggested menus ranging from those for *ospiti di confidenza* (well-known guests or friends) to those for *ospiti di rigurdo* (distinguished guests).

The Lisa Biondi books in their red display box took a prized place on Mamma's kitchen shelf. I loved leafing through them. There are six volumes, starting with appetisers, moving to first courses, eggs and fish, meats, vegetables and ending in cakes. Each page has three or four recipes. The photos are very retro, with close-ups of dishes taken front-on with typical colours of the era – brown, orange, and the occasional splash of red or yellow. I would look longingly at the more complex dishes, like *Sformato di polenta della bisnonna* (a polenta tower with a layered filling of mushrooms and sweetmeat wrapped in slices of prosciutto), *Tortino di crepes* (a tall stack of crepes with layers of meaty ragù and cheese) and *Charlotte di mele* (an unlikely flaming tower of apples, bread and apricot jam, set alight with rum just before serving), wishing Mamma could make these. There are also many less dramatic everyday recipes which, in writing this book and poring over the Lisa Biondi books in detail, I found Mamma based several of her recipes on.

Lisa Biondi first appeared in the 1960s as a home cook who gave advice and recipes, often promoting food products or brands. There was never a photo

> **"**
> **I would suggest the most improbable dishes, for which we did not have most ingredients, and she would laugh and turn the page to a more practical dish ...**

of her, but an illustration where, it has been written, she looked a bit like Grace Kelly. A trusted cook who wrote books and published recipes in magazines, Lisa Biondi was long lived, her recipes appearing well into the 2000s – but she was, as I found out recently, not real. You could think of her as an Italian version of the American home cooking authority Betty Crocker. Lisa Biondi was several people over the years, who wrote recipes sold under this banner. This also explains why her name appears in inverted commas on the books.

The six 'Lisa Biondi' books, which you can still find online second hand, are somewhat dated, but I love them. Many of the basic dishes are excellent, and you will find several versions of them through this book. They remind me of Sunday mornings in the kitchen with Mamma when I still lived at home. We would plan what dishes we would make for Sunday lunch, which was always the most important meal of the week. I would suggest the most improbable dishes, for which we did not have most ingredients, and she would laugh and turn the page to a more practical dish, or else make one of our favourites that she had committed to memory – and there were many of these. Cooking Italian food came easy to her. She knew what went with what, and how much of everything was needed. She made the dishes with love and confidence. And yes, she should have opened that restaurant!

Mamma would cook two *polpettoni*, or meat loaves, at a time and sit them side by side in her electric frying pan. Having a square pan made it much easier to turn the logs over without risking them breaking or cracking, as they were pretty much as long as the pan was. That said, I use a round frying pan and a couple of large spatulas to help me, and I find this works just as well. The strained pan juices make the most delicious sauce, to be poured over the *polpettone* when serving.

Thank you to my sister Barbara for helping me with this recipe.

Italian meatloaf with eggs

POLPETTONE

SERVES 4–6

3 eggs, at room temperature

1 slice of bread

60 ml (¼ cup) milk

1 small zucchini (courgette)

½ carrot, grated

3 French shallots, finely
  chopped

1 garlic clove, finely chopped

2 tablespoons parsley leaves,
  finely chopped

80 g (2¾ oz) black olives with
  pits, or 60 g (2 oz) pitted,
  finely chopped

70 g (2½ oz) parmesan, grated

30 g (1 oz) pancetta, finely
  chopped

500 g (1 lb 2 oz) minced
  (ground) beef

¾ teaspoon salt

1–2 tablespoons dried
  breadcrumbs (only
  use if needed)

3 tablespoons extra virgin
  olive oil

60 ml (¼ cup) dry white wine

Hard-boil two of the eggs by placing them in a small saucepan of water and gently bringing to the boil. Once the water is boiling, cover the pan and turn off the heat. Allow the eggs to sit in the hot water for 10 minutes, then drain. Give the eggs a shake in the pan to crack the shells. When cool enough to handle, carefully peel the eggs and set aside.

Remove the crusts from the bread. Place the bread in a shallow bowl with the milk to soak for a minute, then squeeze to remove the excess milk. Crumble or tear the bread into a large bowl. Coarsely grate the zucchini, squeeze out the excess water and add to the bowl, along with the carrot, shallot, garlic, parsley, olives, parmesan and pancetta.

Add the beef to the bowl, along with the remaining egg. Sprinkle with the salt and plenty of freshly cracked black pepper, then mix with your hands until everything is homogenous. If the mixture seems a bit wet, add some of the dried breadcrumbs.

Lay most of the meat mixture flat on a large sheet of foil on your work surface; the mince should measure about 20 cm × 16 cm (8 inches × 6¼ inches). Lay the hard-boiled eggs in the centre, with a space of 1–2 cm (½–¾ inch) between them, then place some of the leftover meat mixture in that space, packing it tightly. Carefully and firmly roll up the polpettone using the foil to help you to form a log about 20 cm (8 inch) long, using all the spare meat mixture to patch up any areas that need it.

Warm the olive oil in a large, shallow, heavy-based lidded pan, at least 28 cm (11 inches) in diameter. (You want the pan to be large enough to easily turn the polpettone over, without lifting it up.) Turn the heat to medium–low.

Carefully lower the polpettone into the pan and leave it untouched for 10 minutes to brown underneath. Carefully roll it over using two large spatulas and continue browning. If you turn it over too quickly, or have the heat too high, you risk cracks forming and the polpettone breaking into pieces. The polpettone may look squarish or triangular during the browning stage, but will eventually become more log-like. Repeat until browned all over; this takes about 30 minutes in total.

Once browned all over, pour the wine into the pan. When that starts simmering, cover and cook for another 45–55 minutes, turning the polpettone occasionally, until cooked through. Take the lid off for the last 5 minutes or so, to allow any excess liquid to evaporate. You want there to be a bit of liquid, to form a delicious sauce that can be strained and poured over the sliced polpettone.

Once cooked, allow the polpettone to sit in the pan for 15 minutes, then carefully transfer to a chopping board to slice.

Serve thick slices on a bed of spinach (see page 81) or with mashed potatoes, drizzled with the saucy juices. The meatloaf is also really lovely the next day at room temperature.

Opposite: Livia to the far right eating freshly collected clams, Port Philip Bay, Melbourne (1951).

This page: In the original kitchen of the house in Vermont South, Melbourne (1991).

Mamma's sister, Clara, and her husband, Mario, visited us from Italy twice in the 1970s and 1980s. They loved staying at my parents' home with its big backyard, vegetable garden and wine cellar. Mamma and Clara spent lots of time in the kitchen chatting, cooking and trying to make up for the many years they had spent apart. *Zia* Clara introduced some new recipes to Mamma, some of them written on slips of paper, which I found between the pages of old recipe books or in Mamma's recipe bag. This is one such recipe, called 'Brasato Clara'. Clara had written down three ingredients: beef pieces, onions, wine. And one instruction: the same amount of meat as onions.

I remember Mamma making it well beyond 1980, following the same mantra: the same amount of onions and beef. The onions are cooked slowly and almost completely melt into the juices of the meat, wine and beef stock. My version has a few more ingredients than Clara's pared-down recipe. It is a warming dish with a deliciously savoury taste, with a hint of sweetness from the onions.

Clara's slow-cooked beef stew

BRASATO DELLA ZIA CLARA

SERVES 4–6

800 g (1 lb 12 oz) boneless beef
    shoulder, diced into 5 cm
    (2 inch) chunks
2 scant teaspoons salt
4 large white or brown onions
2 tablespoons extra virgin
    olive oil
40 g (1½ oz) unsalted butter
125 ml (½ cup) good-quality
    red wine
125 ml (½ cup) homemade
    or good-quality beef stock,
    plus a few tablespoons
    extra if needed
1 tablespoon tomato paste
    (concentrated puree)
4 sage leaves
1 bay leaf

Place the beef pieces in a bowl. Rub the salt into the beef and set aside while you prepare the onions.

Peel the onions and slice into rings about 3 mm (⅛ inch) thick, then cut each ring in half. Set aside.

Warm the olive oil and butter in a large heavy-based saucepan over medium–low heat for a few minutes. Turn the heat to medium–high and add the beef. Brown on all sides, stirring frequently, for about 3 minutes.

Turn the heat up to high and add the wine. Cook, stirring frequently, for about 3 minutes, until most of the wine evaporates. Reduce the heat to medium and add the onion slices and stock. Stir well and allow to heat through, then add the tomato paste and herbs.

Once the mixture starts bubbling, reduce the heat to low, so the sauce simmers gently. Cover and simmer for at least 1½ hours. Stir occasionally and add extra stock if it looks too dry. The cooking time will depend on the size of the pieces of beef, so larger pieces may take about 2 hours. They should be melt-in-your-mouth tender. Season with salt and freshly cracked black pepper to taste.

Serve the stew with the wine that you used to make it, on a bed of polenta, potato gnocchi or mashed potatoes.

SWEET THINGS

1. Thin almond & lemon biscotti
2. Cinnamon amaretti
3. Buttery almond crescents
4. Old-fashioned coconut & almond slice
5. Crostata with jam
6. Roasted peaches with amaretti & Marsala
7. Vanilla panna cotta with strawberries
8. Livia's Italian trifle
9. Apple & ricotta strudel
10. Isa's pear cake
11. Orange cake with apricots
12. Hazelnut & chocolate layer cake
13. Night & day cake
14. Chocolate & hazelnut log
15. Amaretti & chocolate semifreddo
16. Apricot jam
17. Red plum jam

Biscotti, in literal terms, means 'twice cooked' – which is exactly how these thin biscuits are made. A log of sweet dough studded with almonds is cooked once, left to cool, then thinly sliced and baked again. I love adding lemon zest to Mamma's recipe. You can experiment with different citrus zests and/or extracts. Orange zest and aniseed extract is lovely, or try a combination of lime, orange and lemon zest.

Biscotti are made for dunking! Coffee is great, but wine is even better.

Thin almond & lemon biscotti

BISCOTTI DI MANDORLE CON LIMONE

MAKES 40–60

250 g (9 oz) blanched whole almonds
350 g (2⅓ cups) plain (all-purpose) flour, plus extra for dusting
1½ teaspoons baking powder
180 g (6½ oz) sugar
¼ teaspoon fine sea salt
3 eggs
zest of 1 lemon
2 teaspoons pure vanilla extract
1 teaspoon pure almond extract

Preheat the oven to 140°C (285°F) fan-forced. Line a baking tray with baking paper.

Place the almonds, flour, baking powder, sugar and salt in a bowl and stir to combine.

Break the eggs into a jug. Add the lemon zest and extracts and whisk to combine.

Make a well in the centre of the flour mixture and pour in the egg. Stir with a spoon, and then with your hands, until well combined and homogenous. The dough will be quite thick.

Divide the dough into two even logs, about 18 cm (7 inches) long, using extra flour as needed to shape them. Place them on the baking tray, spacing them well apart. Bake for 35–40 minutes, until pale golden and cooked through.

Turn the oven off and leave the logs to cool completely on a wire rack. This may take an hour or more; you could even leave the second baking until the next day.

When ready for the second baking, preheat the oven to 140°C (285°F) fan-forced. Line several baking trays with baking paper.

Using a large sharp knife, carefully cut the cooled logs into slices about 4–5 mm (¼ inch) thick. Place the biscotti on the baking trays and bake for about 20 minutes, or until firm and golden; the baking time will depend on how thick you have sliced them. Leave to cool on wire racks; the biscotti will become firm as they cool.

The biscotti will keep in a sealed container in the pantry for up to 1 week, or can be frozen for at least 1 month.

I have taken the liberty of adding cinnamon to my mother's recipe. It gives these soft, chewy amaretti an additional warmth, which I just love. When I have egg whites left over from making custard, I often make a double batch and pop most of them in a sealed bag in the freezer. I take one or two out of the freezer, and after about 15 minutes at room temperature they are ready to be dunked in my mid-morning coffee.

Cinnamon amaretti

AMARETTI CON CANNELLA

MAKES ABOUT 18

2 large egg whites
pinch of fine sea salt
200 g (7 oz) almond flour
170 g (¾ cup) caster (superfine) sugar
1 teaspoon ground cinnamon
½ teaspoon pure vanilla extract
flaked, whole or blanched almonds, for decorating

Preheat the oven to 160°C (320°F) fan-forced. Line a large baking tray with baking paper.

Using a hand whisk, beat the egg whites in a bowl with the salt until they just turn white and are foaming.

Place the almond flour, sugar and cinnamon in a large bowl and whisk to combine. Carefully fold through the vanilla extract and beaten egg whites.

Shape the dough into balls about the size of a large walnut. (If the dough is a bit too soft to roll, add a little more almond flour, or even some plain/all-purpose flour.)

Place the dough balls on the baking tray, spaced about 4 cm (1½ inches) apart. Flatten the top slightly with your thumb and decorate with almonds.

Bake for 20–22 minutes, until lightly golden. Leave to cool on wire racks.

The amaretti will keep in a sealed container in the pantry for up to 1 week, or can be frozen for at least 1 month.

This is another recipe my mother continued making until she moved into aged care. She would give these crescents, known as *chifel* (pronounced kee-fel), a good dusting of icing sugar while they were still warm, using a green metal sifter she bought in the early 1950s. The sifter made a slight scraping sound when the handle was squeezed, rotating the internal wheel backwards and forwards to release a shower of icing sugar. I loved hearing this sound growing up; it meant something deliciously sweet was about to emerge from the kitchen.

Buttery almond crescents

CHIFEL DI MANDORLE

MAKES 25

300 g (2 cups) plain
    (all-purpose) flour, plus
    extra for dusting
150 g (5½ oz) almond flour
100 g (3½ oz) caster (superfine)
    sugar
a good pinch of fine sea salt
250 g (9 oz) butter, softened
1 teaspoon pure vanilla extract
icing (confectioners') sugar,
    for dusting

Line two baking trays with baking paper.

Place the flour, almond flour, caster sugar and salt in a large wide bowl and give a good whisk to combine. Add the butter and vanilla and stir with a large spoon, then bring the dough together with your hands.

Break off 30 g (1 oz) chunks, about the size of a small apricot, and roll each one, on a lightly floured surface, into a 10 cm (4 inch) long rope. If the dough is too soft to work with, place in the fridge for 15 minutes to firm up. Form each rope into a horseshoe shape that's slightly fatter in the middle and place on the baking trays.

Place the baking trays in the fridge for 15–30 minutes for the crescents to firm up.

Meanwhile, preheat the oven to 160°C (320°F) fan-forced.

Transfer the baking trays to the oven and bake the crescents for 18–20 minutes, until lightly golden. Remove from the oven and leave to cool on the trays for 5 minutes, then carefully lift off the crescents and place on a wire rack.

While they are still warm, dust the crescents with icing sugar. Leave to cool to room temperature; they will firm up as they cool.

The crescents will keep in a sealed container in the pantry for up to a week.

Frescoed wall, Verona (2022).

By the time Mamma turned 90, she had stopped making many sweet treats, with two exceptions – the almond crescents on page 157, and her 'slice' (she used the word in English, even when speaking Italian), using a recipe from a dog-eared copy of the *Australian Women's Weekly Cakes and Slices Cookbook* published in 1987. She used a square gold-coloured baking tin, its base well-marked by the dozens and dozens of times she made the slice, cutting it into small squares using a sharp pointed knife. She would pop the squares in a freezer bag, taking out a couple whenever one of the grandchildren dropped in. When she passed away and I inherited the cookbooks, it took a bit of searching to find out which of the many slices was the one she would make. My daughter, Tamara, and I went through them and decided it was a caramel walnut slice, which Tamara believes she made with almond flour, rather than walnuts.

This version comes pretty close to hers, featuring a deliciously chewy almond topping with a hint of caramel on a firm coconut biscuit base.

Old-fashioned coconut & almond slice

'SLICE' DI COCCO E MANDORLE

MAKES 24 SQUARES

120 g (4½ oz) butter, melted, plus extra for greasing
120 g (4½ oz) plain (all-purpose) flour
100 g (3½ oz) fine desiccated or shredded coconut
90 g (3 oz) sugar
a good pinch of fine sea salt
1 teaspoon baking powder

For the topping
100 g (3½ oz) brown sugar
50 g (1¾ oz) shredded coconut
50 g (1¾ oz) almond flour
2 eggs, lightly beaten
1 teaspoon pure almond extract
a good pinch of fine sea salt

Preheat the oven to 170°C (340°F) fan-forced. Grease a 23 cm (9 inch) square tin with butter and line the base and sides with baking paper, leaving the paper hanging over the edge, to help with un-moulding.

Combine the flour, coconut, sugar and salt in a bowl and whisk lightly to combine. Pour in the melted butter and mix until combined. Press the mixture firmly into the base of the tin, to cover the entire base. Bake for 15 minutes.

Place all the topping ingredients in a large bowl and mix with a spoon until homogenous. Spread onto the cooked base and bake for a further 25 minutes. Remove from the oven and allow the slice to cool in the tin, before cutting into squares.

The slice will keep in a sealed container in the pantry for several days, or can be frozen for up to 1 month.

The simplest of all my mother's cakes and tarts, crostata makes good use of all the jam we had in the pantry. My school friend Jo, who came over most weekends to play, often recounts her memory of our crostata. Mamma would reach up to the high shelf of the pantry and, as if by magic, reveal a perfectly latticed crostata, made with apricot or plum jam for our afternoon tea.

Crostata with jam

CROSTATA DI MARMELLATA

SERVES 8-10

140 g (5 oz) unsalted butter, chilled, plus extra butter for greasing

280 g (10 oz) plain (all-purpose) flour, plus extra for dusting

50 g (1¾ oz) sugar

¼ teaspoon fine sea salt

zest of ½ lemon

1 teaspoon pure vanilla extract

1 egg, cold from the fridge

1-2 teaspoons chilled water

370 g (13 oz) Apricot jam (see page 198) or Red plum jam (see page 202), chilled

Cut the butter into small dice and place in the fridge until ready to use.

Grease the base and side of a 28 cm (11 inch) round loose-based flan (tart) tin with butter. Line the base with baking paper.

Place the flour, sugar, salt and butter in a food processor. Pulse until the mixture resembles coarse sand. Add the lemon zest and vanilla. With the motor going, break in the egg and add enough chilled water until the pastry comes together and forms a ball. Tip onto a well-floured work surface and knead briefly to shape the ball into a disc. Break off one-third of the pastry, roll into a thick strip, wrap in baking paper and place in the fridge. Roll the remaining two-thirds of the pastry into a 32 cm (12½ inch) circle, about 3-4 mm (⅛ inch) thick.

Using the rolling pin to help you, lift the pastry over your tart tin and press it into the base and side of the tin. You will need to work fairly quickly, or the butter will soften too much. Trim the side so it sits about 1 cm (½ inch) above the pastry base, reserving the pastry scraps for the lattice top, if needed. Cover the tin with a clean cloth, then place in the fridge to chill.

Remove the remaining pastry third from the fridge and roll out on a well-floured surface to a thickness of 3-4 mm (⅛ inch). Cut into 10 strips, about 1.5 cm (½ inch) wide; you may need to re-roll your pastry scraps a few times. Some strips should be longer and some shorter for the lattice on your tart.

Preheat the oven to 160°C (320°F) fan-forced while you assemble the crostata.

Remove the tart tin from the fridge and evenly spread the jam over the base; I like to cut any larger pieces of fruit that I find in the jam. Next, make a lattice pattern with the pastry strips, trimming the excess.

Bake for 40-45 minutes, or until the pastry has turned golden. Remove from the oven and leave to cool before releasing the tart from the tin.

The crostata will keep in an airtight container in the pantry for 3-4 days.

AN INSTAGRAM NONNA

I started my Instagram page at the end of 2011, when it was a brand-new photo-sharing application. My niece Claire first showed me the app during our Christmas Day lunch that year and introduced me, virtually, to her food blogger friends who were already on there. My interest was piqued and I took the name @italyonmymind – the same as the food blog I had recently started. I quickly made a small group of Instagram friends, with a common love of Italy and food, taking and sharing photos of my meals. Soon after, my mother became part of the conversation.

Once my father passed away, my sister and I made a point of regularly visiting Mamma for lunch. She derived great joy in cooking for us now that she was alone, and wouldn't hear of us coming at any other time of day. I would ring the doorbell and Mamma would call out *Ze verto!* (It's open!) Warm and delicious smells filled the entrance hall and a beaming Mamma would greet me. Lunch preparation would be well underway. After saying hello, I would approach the stovetop to taste whatever was cooking, while she shooed me away telling me not to ruin my appetite before lunch.

We would chat and, before too long, lunch was ready to be served. I would take out my phone with its camera and quickly snap away at the plates of food. Once we started eating, I would tell her to stop and take another photo, trying to catch her hands in the image. Then we would eat cake or biscuits with coffee and play Scopa with Italian cards, and I'd take more photos. At the table she would tell her stories from long ago in dialect and occasionally in English, and I would film them.

Later I would post photos of our lunch or snippets of the videos on Instagram with the hashtag #lunchwithmammalivia. If you have a look on Instagram you will see many photos of Mamma, our meals, our card games and her hands. People loved the food she prepared, the familiarity of the dishes, the placemats and the table setting, her often animated expressions and her sweet smile.

Mamma seemed to delight in the fact that I wanted to take photos of our lunches. Over time, she started posing, dutifully holding a fork or reaching for a plate

> **"**
> **People loved the food she prepared, the familiarity of the dishes, the placemats and the table setting, her often animated expressions and her sweet smile.**

with her hand and waiting for me to click my phone camera before starting the meal. I don't think she really grasped what she was part of, or how people from the other side of the world were liking the images and commenting with real connection to what they were seeing. She was my mother, but in the eyes of many, because of her age, she was a nonna – an Instagram nonna long before many others.

In early 2016, Lisa Valmorbida, the owner of Melbourne gelateria Pidapipó, got in touch with me. She was developing a gelato campaign for Mother's Day, with the focus being on nonne (grandmothers); could my mother, Livia, be part of the campaign? Claire and I were more excited than my mother, who didn't seem to grasp what this was about. Lisa developed the Nonna Bacchia gelato with zesty ricotta, pine nuts and grappa, which was based on Mamma's ricotta cake recipe, to be sold for the week around Mother's Day. I took Mamma to the promotional photoshoot, where there were two other nonne who had gelati named after them: Nonna Corso and Nonna Valmorbida. To my mother's great surprise, Lisa's grandmother was Elsie, a friend from the 1960s who she had lost touch with. When they met in the gelateria, they hugged, tears in their eyes, and held hands while we took photos of them eating gelato.

It was a joyous reunion of nonne, all made possible by an app called Instagram.

When they retired in the 1990s, my parents made the big decision to renovate the kitchen. It was designed so that Mamma would finally have the light-filled space she had longed for; out went the mission brown tiles and orange Laminex, and in their place pale-blue benchtops and blond-wood trims. Mamma loved her bright and spacious new kitchen and this was the scene that framed our meals and the Instagram photos at the hashtag #lunchwithmammalivia.

My mother had a love affair with amaretti. As well as the chewy ones she loved to make (see page 154), there were the crisp light-as-a-feather ones that were sold in packets. They are delicious dunked in a cup of coffee, or crushed to make a crumble to scatter over ice cream – but in roasted stuffed peaches they are divine. You can serve half a peach per person, or two peach halves, depending on the appetite of your guests.

Roasted peaches with amaretti & Marsala

PESCHE AL FORNO CON AMARETTI E MARSALA

SERVES 4-8

4 large clingstone yellow
    peaches
1 smaller yellow peach
3 tablespoons brown sugar
3 tablespoons finely chopped
    almonds
45 g (1½ oz) unsalted butter, at
    room temperature
1 teaspoon vanilla bean paste
a small pinch of fine sea salt
8 store-bought amaretti
90 ml (3 fl oz) Marsala
vanilla bean ice cream, to serve

Preheat the oven to 160°C (320°F) fan-forced. Line a rimmed baking tray with baking paper.

Cut the peaches in half vertically, from the stemmed top to the base. Twist the two halves in opposite directions to prise them apart. Remove the stone from the half where it is attached, plus a good teaspoon of peach flesh beneath the stone. Remove about the same amount from the other peach half, so you have a large cavity for the filling. Finely chop the scooped-out peach flesh and place in a bowl.

Remove the stone from the small peach, then peel off the skin with a sharp knife. Finely chop the flesh and add to the bowl, along with the sugar, almonds, butter, vanilla bean paste and salt. Crush four of the amaretti into the bowl and mix with a spoon until homogenous.

Place the peach halves, cut side up, fairly snugly on the baking tray. Spoon the filling into the peach cavities.

Bake for 40 minutes. Remove the tray from the oven, pour the Marsala over the peaches and onto the tray, then bake for a further 15 minutes. The peaches are ready when they are easily pierced with a skewer, and the Marsala in the base of the tray has reduced to a syrup. If it hasn't, pour it into a small saucepan and reduce it on the stovetop.

Serve the warm peach halves with a scoop of vanilla bean ice cream, pouring the syrup on top just before serving, and topping with the remaining crushed amaretti.

As a child, it fascinated me how the strawberries in juice that Mamma made tasted even more like strawberries than the fruit on its own. And her trick was so simple that she soon had me doing it – leaving the strawberries to marinate for a few hours in a mix of citrus juices with a dash of sugar. They were equally delightful cold from the fridge or at room temperature, and on their own or over ice cream or whipped sweetened cream. The creamy part was simply a vehicle for the strawberries and their ruby-coloured nectar.

This recipe makes a lot more strawberries than you need for the panna cotta cups, so you can halve the quantity if you like – but they are so delicious, you will find yourself eating them by the spoonful from the bowl.

Vanilla panna cotta with strawberries

PANNA COTTA CON LE FRAGOLE

SERVES 4

1⅛ titanium gelatine leaves
500 ml (2 cups) pouring cream
70 g (2½ oz) sugar
1 teaspoon vanilla bean paste
500 g (1 lb 2 oz) strawberries
juice of 1 orange
juice of 1 lemon
2–3 teaspoons caster
    (superfine) sugar

You will need to make the panna cotta at least 6 hours before serving, to give it time to set.

Place the gelatine leaves in a bowl of cold water for at least 10 minutes to soften.

In a saucepan, slowly heat the cream, sugar and vanilla bean paste, stirring occasionally to dissolve the sugar. Heat until almost boiling – but don't let the mixture boil. Turn off the heat and set aside.

Remove the gelatine leaves from the water and give them a gentle squeeze to remove the water. Drop them into the hot cream and stir until dissolved and completely smooth.

Allow the cream to cool for about 10 minutes, before carefully pouring it into four serving glasses, at least 150 ml (5 fl oz) in capacity. (Make sure the cream isn't too hot, or the glasses may crack.) Cover all the glasses so nothing falls in them. Allow to cool to room temperature, then place in the fridge for at least 6 hours.

About 2 hours before serving, prepare the strawberries. Rinse and drain well, then remove the hulls. Cut in half, or into quarters if large, and place in a bowl. Strain the lemon and orange juice into the bowl. Add the caster sugar to taste, then stir and set aside to marinate.

Serve the panna cotta straight from the fridge, topped with as many strawberries as you like.

This recipe was a dinner party favourite in the 1970s. On the rare occasions that it wasn't all eaten on the Saturday night, I would sneak spoonfuls of leftovers on a Sunday morning straight from the fridge. Mamma went through a phase of Australianising the recipe by adding a layer of red jelly and changing the name to *traifel*. We protested that the original was much better, and she eventually stopped adding the layer of red – but she still called it trifle!

You will need a decorative serving bowl for this dish. The one I use has a capacity of about 1.5 litres (6 cups).

Livia's Italian trifle

ZUPPA INGLESE

SERVES 8–10

750 ml (3 cups) milk
1 teaspoon vanilla bean paste
6 egg yolks
170 g (6 oz) sugar
80 g (2¾ oz) cornflour
(cornstarch)
pinch of sea salt
75 g (2¾ oz) dark chocolate
(40% cocoa solids), roughly
chopped, plus extra grated
or shaved chocolate for
topping
125–185 ml (½–¾ cup) Marsala
150 g (5½ oz) store-bought
savoiardi (ladyfinger/
sponge finger biscuits)

Pour the milk into a saucepan. Add the vanilla paste and slowly bring to just below boiling point.

While the milk is heating, whisk the egg yolks and sugar in a large bowl, using an electric mixer (or vigorously by hand), until the mixture is thick and creamy. Sift in the cornflour and salt and whisk until incorporated. Pour in the hot milk in a slow, thin stream, whisking as you go.

Scrape the mixture back into the saucepan and return to the heat. Continue to warm the custard slowly, stirring continuously with a spatula. You want the custard to thicken so that it coats the back of a spoon, becomes visibly thicker and more difficult to stir; this can take up to 20 minutes. I keep a metal hand whisk handy while I'm doing this, in case the custard starts thickening unevenly, so I can give it a bit of a whisk to smooth it out. If you like your custard thick (I like mine a little runny in this dessert), cook it a little longer.

Have two bowls ready for the custard, and place the chopped chocolate in one of them. Pour half the custard into each bowl, stirring it into the chocolate until melted and homogenous. Set aside to cool slightly.

Pour the Marsala into a shallow bowl that you can fully dunk the savoiardi in. Briefly dip half the biscuits into the Marsala, then lay them one by one on the base of your serving bowl, covering the entire base, breaking some into smaller pieces to fill any gaps.

Pour all the chocolate custard over the biscuit layer, to cover them. Make another layer of savoiardi in the same way, then pour the vanilla custard over them. Pat down with a spatula or spoon so the top is smooth. Cover and refrigerate for at least 4 hours, or even overnight; it will keep for up to 48 hours. Serve sprinkled with extra grated or shaved chocolate.

My aunt Clara had no children of her own and was much loved by us all. I remember hugging her crocheted blue woollen shawl for days after she had left Australia to fly back home to Italy, her familiar scent bringing memories of her flooding back. She was generous to a fault, warm, funny and mischievous. She loved to cook and Mamma added several of Clara's recipes to her repertoire. This recipe for apple and ricotta strudel is one of hers.

You could make your own strudel pastry, but sometimes it is so much easier to use good-quality, all-butter store-bought puff pastry.

Apple & ricotta strudel

STRUDEL DI RICOTTA E MELE DI CLARA

SERVES 8-10

4 granny smith apples, 800 g
    (1 lb 12 oz) in total
60 g (2 oz) butter
100 g (3½ oz) sugar
250 g (1 cup) ricotta
½ teaspoon pure vanilla extract
375 g (13 oz) store-bought puff
    pastry
zest of 1 lemon
30 g (1 oz) pine nuts, toasted
60 g (½ cup) sultanas (golden
    raisins), soaked in white
    rum, grappa or hot water
30 g (1 oz) dried breadcrumbs
1 egg yolk
a dash of milk

Peel and core the apples, then cut into 3–4 cm (1¼–1½ inch) chunks. In a frying pan large enough to fit all the apple pieces, melt the butter over medium heat. Toss in the apple pieces and scatter 40 g (1½ oz) of the sugar over. Cover and cook, stirring occasionally, until the apple pieces soften but still retain their shape. How long this takes depends on their size – anywhere from 8 to 15 minutes. Remove the lid for the last few minutes so that most of the liquid evaporates. Set aside to cool.

Drain the ricotta, then place in a bowl with the vanilla and remaining sugar. Stir well, until the sugar is well incorporated and the ricotta is smooth and spreadable.

Preheat the oven to 200°C (400°F) fan-forced. Line a large baking tray with baking paper. Thaw the pastry according to the packet instructions.

On a large sheet of baking paper, roll the pastry out to a rectangle, about 42 cm × 30 cm (16½ inches × 12 inches). You will be rolling up the strudel on its long edge to form a sausage about 40 cm (15¾ inches) in length.

Spread the ricotta mixture on most of the pastry, leaving a 10 cm (4 inch) margin on one long edge, and a 1 cm (½ inch) margin on the other three sides. Evenly scatter on the cooled apple, the lemon zest, pine nuts, drained sultanas and breadcrumbs. Carefully roll the strudel up, using the baking paper to help you. Seal the ends by folding over and pressing down.

Slip the strudel onto the baking tray. Using a sharp knife, make four or five incisions, 5–7 cm (2–2¾ inches) long, on top of the strudel, either across or diagonally, to allow air to escape during baking. Lightly whisk the egg yolk and milk and brush over the top of the strudel.

Bake for 15 minutes, then reduce the oven temperature to 180°C (350°F) and bake for a further 25–30 minutes, until the top of the pastry is nicely golden.

Remove from the oven and leave to rest for about 15 minutes before slicing. Serve warm or at room temperature, on its own, or with a dollop of cream or vanilla ice cream.

The strudel will keep in a sealed container in the fridge for about 2 days; gently reheat for serving.

Opposite: Freshly picked backyard lemons,
Vermont South (2017).

This page: Next to the newly constructed house in
Station Street, Box Hill South, Melbourne (1954).

Mamma learnt this cake from Isa at the Italian social club she and my father would frequent when they had retired. The women were usually in the kitchen at the club, which was a school hall, cooking dinner and chatting. The men were in the other rooms, playing cards and discussing politics. I went with them a few times and do not think I ever saw one of the husbands in the kitchen helping to prepare the meal!

Isa's recipe was with apples, but my mother would occasionally switch to pears, or a combination of pears and apples. I love the pear version best. The dusting of raw sugar just before baking makes a lovely firm and sugary crust on top of the cake.

Isa's pear cake

TORTA DI PERE ISA

SERVES 8-10

4 large beurre bosc pears, about 900 g (2 lb) in total
180 g (6½ oz) self-raising flour
110 g (½ cup) sugar
½ teaspoon ground cinnamon
zest of 1 lemon
a good pinch of sea salt
2 eggs
120 ml (4 fl oz) light olive oil or grapeseed oil
60 ml (¼ cup) milk
1 teaspoon pure vanilla extract
1 generous tablespoon raw sugar

Preheat the oven to 160°C (320°F) fan-forced. Grease the base and side of a 21 cm (8¼ inch) round loose-based cake tin and line with baking paper.

Peel and core the pears. Cut into quarters, slice lengthways into segments, then chop the segments in half. Set aside in a bowl.

Place the flour, sugar, cinnamon, lemon zest and salt in a bowl. Whisk to combine.

In a second bowl, whisk the eggs, oil, milk and vanilla to combine. Pour into the flour mixture and stir until well combined. Tip the pears in and gently fold through the batter.

Pour the whole lot into the cake tin and smooth the top with the back of a spoon. Scatter the raw sugar evenly over the top.

Bake for 15 minutes, then reduce the oven temperature to 150°C (300°F) and bake for a further 40–45 minutes, until golden on top and cooked through.

Remove from the oven and allow to cool in the tin for 10 minutes. Enjoy warm, or at room temperature. The cake will keep in a sealed container in a cool spot for up to 3 days.

There was always a cake on the go at home. You never knew when friends would unexpectedly drop by, and it would not be very Italian to not offer them food, preferably homemade. Jam crostata (see page 162) was an easy option that could comfortably sit in the pantry for a few days, waiting for the doorbell to ring. Another cake that was on high rotation in the 1980s and 1990s was a simple orange and coconut cake that Mamma baked in a loaf (bar) tin. It is somewhat less Italian than crostata, but Mamma found a way to make it her own by adding fruit to the batter. I found this handwritten recipe in the recipe bag she kept in the kitchen cupboard; it has apricots through it and is really quite delicious. It makes a lovely breakfast cake.

Orange cake with apricots

TORTA ARANCIA E COCCO CON ALBICOCCHE

SERVES 8-10

125 g (4½ oz) unsalted butter, at room temperature
200 g (7 oz) caster (superfine) sugar
2 large eggs
250 g (1⅔ cups) plain (all-purpose) flour
40 g (1½ oz) desiccated or shredded coconut
2 teaspoons baking powder
a good pinch of sea salt
zest of 1 orange
130 ml (4½ fl oz) orange juice
5 large apricots

Preheat the oven to 160°C (320°F) fan-forced. Line the base and side of a 22 cm (8¾ inch) round loose-based cake tin.

Cream the butter and sugar in a bowl, using an electric mixer, until pale and creamy. Add the eggs, one at a time, and beat until pale and fluffy. Fold the flour, coconut, baking powder and salt through, along with the orange zest and orange juice.

Cut two of the apricots into small pieces and fold through the batter. Pour into the cake tin.

Halve or quarter the remaining apricots and decorate the top of the cake, cut side up, pushing them slightly into the batter with your fingers.

Bake for 1 hour or until the cake is a deep golden colour and a skewer inserted into the centre comes out clean.

Remove from the oven and allow to cool in the tin. Serve at room temperature.

The cake will keep in a sealed container in the pantry for up to 3 days.

This was my aunt Clara's celebration cake. When she came to Australia, she brought the recipe with her and it became my father's favourite celebratory cake. She would make it for birthdays and take it to friends and family as a birthday gift. When you discover how good it is, you may not want to give it away like Clara did! It also happens to be gluten free.

Hazelnut & chocolate layer cake

TORTA CORNELIA

SERVES 12-16

7 eggs (about 60 g/2 oz each)
250 g (9 oz) sugar
380 g (13½ oz) hazelnut flour
1 teaspoon pure vanilla extract
2 pinches of sea salt

Chocolate icing
3 eggs
190 g (6½ oz) sugar
110 g (4 oz) dark chocolate
    (45% cocoa solids),
    broken into squares
190 g (6½ oz) unsalted butter,
    at room temperature

To finish
80 ml (⅓ cup) cold espresso
    coffee
40 ml (1¼ fl oz) white rum
crushed hazelnuts
shaved chocolate

Preheat the oven to 180°C (350°F) fan-forced. Grease the base and side of a 22 cm (8¾ inch) round loose-based cake tin and line with baking paper.

Separate the yolks and whites of six of the eggs. Place the six egg yolks and the remaining whole egg in a bowl with the sugar. Using a stand mixer or hand-held electric mixer, beat at medium–high speed until thick, pale and creamy. Add the hazelnut flour in batches, then the vanilla and a pinch of salt, beating at low speed until well combined.

In a separate bowl, beat the six egg whites with the remaining pinch of salt until medium–firm peaks form.

By hand, mix a tablespoon of the beaten egg white into the cake batter to loosen it a bit. Using a spatula, and working in five or more batches, carefully fold the remaining egg white through the batter, so as not to lose aeration. Carefully pour the batter into the cake tin.

Bake for 10 minutes. Reduce the oven temperature to 160°C (320°F) and bake for a further 30–35 minutes, until a skewer inserted into the centre comes out clean.

Leave the cake in the tin on a wire rack to cool for 10 minutes before unmoulding. Allow to cool to room temperature before proceeding.

Meanwhile, make the icing. Place the eggs and sugar in a heatproof bowl and beat using an electric mixer until creamy and light. Set the bowl over a small saucepan of barely simmering water and add the chocolate, square by square, stirring so that it melts into the egg mixture. Pour the lot into a clean small saucepan and place over very low heat, stirring continuously with a silicone spatula until the mixture thickens – 70–80°C (158–176°F) on a sugar thermometer. Don't allow the temperature to exceed 80°C (176°F), or the eggs will scramble. Remove from the heat and allow to cool to room temperature.

→

When the chocolate mixture has cooled, beat in the room-temperature butter, one cube at a time, until all the butter has been evenly incorporated.

To assemble the cake, use a large serrated knife to slice the cake horizontally into three equal layers. Brush the lower layer with half the coffee, then spread with a layer of icing. Place the next disc of cake on top, then drizzle with the rum and cover with another icing layer. Top with the last cake disc and brush with the remaining coffee. Spread the remaining icing over the top and side of the cake.

Decorate with crushed hazelnuts and shaved chocolate.

Refrigerate for at least 3 hours, or even overnight, before serving.

The cake will keep in a sealed container in the fridge for several days.

Opposite: Farmhouse Gorgo al Monticano, Veneto (2022).
This page: Granddaughter Tamara and Livia (2016).

Giorno e notte literally means 'night and day' and is what my mother called her marble cake - a simple cake that the children, and then the grandchildren, would help her make. There was usually a bit of a fight to see who got the beater with the most batter on it, and who managed to scrape out the side of the bowl of chocolate batter. My mother's recipe had four eggs in it, but I have added yoghurt in place of one of the eggs, to keep the cake moist for longer - not that it lasts that long!

Night & day cake

CIAMBELLA GIORNO E NOTTE

SERVES 8-10

125 g (4½ oz) butter, at room temperature, plus extra for greasing
180 g (6½ oz) self-raising flour, plus extra for dusting
150 g (5½ oz) caster (superfine) sugar
3 large eggs
60 g (2 oz) Greek-style yoghurt
80 ml (⅓ cup) milk, plus an extra 1 tablespoon
zest of 1 lemon
1 teaspoon pure vanilla extract
2 tablespoons bitter (raw unsweetened) cocoa powder
icing (confectioners') sugar, for dusting

Preheat the oven to 160°C (320°F) fan-forced. Butter the sides and base of a ring (bundt) tin, then dust with flour.

Cream the butter and sugar in a bowl, using an electric mixer. Add the eggs, one at a time, beating well after each addition. Add the yoghurt and 80 ml (⅓ cup) of milk and beat gently until incorporated. Fold the flour through until the mixture is homogenous.

Evenly divide the batter between two bowls.

To one bowl, add the lemon zest and vanilla and mix with a spoon until homogenous.

Sift the cocoa powder into the second bowl, add the extra tablespoon of milk and stir well.

Pour about half the chocolate batter into the cake tin, then half the vanilla batter. Then add the remaining chocolate batter and finally the remaining vanilla batter. The idea is to create a marbled pattern of the two batters; it is totally up to you how you pour them into the tin. Give the tin a bit of a bang on the bench to even out the top of the cake batter.

Slip into the oven and bake for 30–35 minutes, until a skewer inserted in the cake comes out clean.

Leave the cake in the tin on a wire rack to cool for a few minutes, then gently bang the tin on the bench a few times to loosen the cake from the tin. Invert the cake onto the rack.

When the cake has cooled to room temperature, dust with icing sugar. The cake will keep in a sealed container in a cool spot for a couple of days.

Chocolate ripple cake is a dessert from my childhood. It was made using Arnott's Choc Ripple biscuits, and if my memory serves me correctly, the recipe was even on the biscuit packet. Mamma always dipped them in Marsala while making the dessert, turning an Australian classic into an Italian hybrid.

The recipe below uses homemade buttery chocolate hazelnut shortbread rounds and is fancy enough to serve at your next retro dinner party. You will have about one-third of the biscuits left over after preparing the recipe, but they are wonderful with coffee.

Chocolate & hazelnut log

TRONCO DI CIOCCOLATA E NOCCIOLE

SERVES 6-8

190 g (6½ oz) plain (all-purpose) flour, plus extra for dusting
110 g (4 oz) hazelnut flour
110 g (4 oz) sugar
25 g (1 oz) bitter (raw unsweetened) cocoa powder, sifted
⅓ teaspoon fine sea salt
160 g (5½ oz) butter, softened
½ teaspoon pure vanilla extract

Vanilla cream
300 ml (10 fl oz) pouring cream
½ teaspoon icing (confectioners') sugar
½ teaspoon pure vanilla extract

To finish
60 ml (¼ cup) Marsala
1 tablespoon grated dark chocolate

Line two baking trays with baking paper.

Whisk together the flour, hazelnut flour, sugar, cocoa powder and salt in a bowl. Using a spoon, stir in the softened butter and vanilla, then bring the dough together with your hands. Knead briefly on your work surface, then break off 25 g (1 oz) balls and flatten into discs, rolling the dough in extra flour if it feels too sticky, and place on the baking trays; you should end up with about 22 discs. Place the trays in the fridge to chill for at least 1 hour.

Preheat the oven to 160°C (320°F) fan-forced. On a floured surface, roll out the discs with a rolling pin and use a biscuit cutter to make 6 cm (2½ inch) circles from the dough discs. Place them back on the baking trays and bake for 18–20 minutes, until they are cooked through and smell delicious. Remove from the oven and allow the biscuits to cool on the trays. Store in a sealed container if not making the log immediately.

Using an electric mixer, whip the vanilla cream ingredients in a bowl until medium–firm peaks form. Smear a tablespoon or two of the cream on the base of a rectangular serving dish. Dip one biscuit into the Marsala, first on one side, then on the other – don't allow it to soak, or it may fall apart. Using a butter knife, place a thick smear of vanilla cream on one biscuit. Join to another Marsala-dipped biscuit, smear that with vanilla cream and stand them on their sides in the serving dish. Repeat, joining one biscuit to the next, until you have 12–14 biscuits along the length of the dish. Decorate the whole log with the remaining vanilla cream.

Cover the log with a large inverted plastic container, to provide a protective layer around the log. Refrigerate for 6 hours, or even overnight, to 'set' the whipped cream.

When ready to serve, sprinkle with the grated dark chocolate. Cut into slices at least one finger thick. Keep in the fridge and eat within 2 days.

Opposite: Granddaughter Claire and Livia (1980).
This page: Figs on Nello's painting (1971).

Nello
1971

I love this recipe, which my aunt Clara used to make during the months she stayed with the family in Australia in the late 1970s. My father declared it was better than ice cream, so from then on Mamma made it on repeat for dinner parties. The texture is slightly chewy, light and creamy. It is not in the least bit icy, like homemade ice cream can sometimes get. You will be hooked, I promise!

You will need a 1.5 litre (6 cup) loaf (bar) or terrine tin for this recipe.

Amaretti & chocolate semifreddo

SEMIFREDDO DELLA ZIA CLARA

SERVES 8-10

3 eggs, separated
130 g (4½ oz) sugar
100 g (3½ oz) store-bought
    crisp amaretti
1 teaspoon pure almond extract
a good pinch of sea salt
500 ml (2 cups) pouring cream
50 g (1¾ oz) dark chocolate
    (45% cocoa solids), grated

To serve
store-bought crisp amaretti
grated dark chocolate
    (45% cocoa solids)
fresh raspberries

Place the egg yolks and sugar in a large bowl and beat using an electric mixer for several minutes, until pale and creamy.

Place the amaretti in a mini food processor and blend to a fine powder. Stir the crushed amaretti and almond extract through the egg yolk mixture.

In a separate bowl, whisk the egg whites and salt until firm peaks form. In a third bowl, beat the cream until stiff peaks form.

Fold the egg whites through the egg yolk mixture in batches, taking care not to lose aeration. Next, working in batches, carefully fold the cream and grated chocolate through.

Carefully line a 1.5 litre (6 cup) loaf or terrine tin with baking paper or plastic wrap, to help you lift out the semifreddo once set. Pour the mixture in, then lightly pat with the back of a large spoon or spatula to flatten.

Cover and freeze for at least 4 hours. To remove the semifreddo from the tin, wet a clean tea towel with hot water and wipe it over the outside of the tin; you want the semifreddo edges to soften slightly, so you can lift it out of the tin. Repeat until you can easily lift the semifreddo out, placing it on a chopping board.

Cut the semifreddo into finger-width slices and place on chilled serving plates. Decorate with crushed amaretti, grated chocolate and fresh raspberries, and serve immediately, with an extra amaretto on each plate.

Don't allow any leftover semifreddo to melt; place it back in the tin, pop it back in the freezer and eat within 3–4 days.

STORIES OF FRUIT & JAM

We had returned to Melbourne, Australia, in the early 1970s, after a failed resettlement in Italy, needing to buy a home with our sadly depleted savings. My father had his heart set on buying a property in the country; he wanted plenty of land to plant vegetables, grow fruit, make wine. However, my mother wouldn't hear of it. We had always lived in a city, and she wanted to be close to the mod cons and in walking distance to her neighbours. As a compromise, we bought a house on a largish corner block in the newly established suburb of Vermont South, in what had previously been orchards. The land had been cleared, though not that thoroughly, as there was a shrub-sized pear tree and an apple tree in our future driveway. And so, in 1973, we purchased the house for the princely sum of $23,500 – the equivalent of over three years' pre-tax salary.

My father set to work creating garden beds and planting a lush fruit garden and a seasonal vegetable orto. There were two lemon trees, three plum trees, a fig tree, one apricot tree, one nectarine tree, one white peach tree and an apple tree left from the orchard. The vegetable garden changed from year to year, alternating combinations of green beans, borlotti beans, potatoes, zucchini (courgettes), eggplants (aubergines), pumpkins (winter squash), silverbeet (Swiss chard), radicchio and garlic – but there were always tomatoes, many different varieties, planted alongside bushes of basil.

In summer, it was all systems go with fruit harvesting, and my mother took to making jam: fig, plum and apricot. Apricot was our favourite, though there was some tension in the kitchen on apricot jam–making day, as my father's mantra was 'don't make the jam too runny'. Mamma kept a book of jam recipes with handwritten notes on the amount of sugar and number of lemons for each type of jam. The aim was to have jams that were not too sweet, and just the right consistency for spreading on bread. All her jams were beautifully set, except for the apricot jam, which most years could be poured out of the jar. My father, who ate jam most days for breakfast, often with ricotta on toast, would mutter, 'It's the pectin, it doesn't have enough pectin,' (pronouncing it 'pec-teen').

> "
> **There were two lemon trees, three plum trees, a fig tree, one apricot tree, one nectarine tree, one white peach tree and an apple tree.**

Pectin helps set the jam and is found in lemons, especially in the pips. So Mamma would add more lemon juice, pulp and pips ... making it too sour. She even tried adding sachets of powdered pectin, which made the jam set ... but gave it an odd metallic taste, and hence it was banned from the kitchen.

I loved the runny apricot jam, and would eat it poured over yoghurt. It also made a lovely fruit compote.

As he got older, my father stopped spraying the trees, being unable to climb the ladder to reach the uppermost branches. The apricot tree became infected with a rust-leaf virus, and the few apricots that would appear were small and mottled. Mamma eventually stopped making apricot jam, but focused her efforts on plum jam – which always turned out beautifully. The plum trees (one Mariposa and two Santa Rosa) produced massive amounts of fruit, even without being sprayed, right up to 2018, when we sold the house in Vermont South and Mamma moved into aged care.

I only recently finished the jars of jam made with the fruit from the plum trees. The last jar went into a lovely latticed jam crostata. As I spooned a thick crimson layer over the pastry base, I thought of Mamma seated in the kitchen, wearing her *traversa* (apron), and the stories she would tell as we chopped the fruit, weighed the sugar and put the lemon pulp and pips into muslin bags in preparation for our annual jam making.

The notes in Mamma's jam-making book can be summarised as follows: Apricot 750 g (1 lb 11 oz) sugar; red or black plums 900 g (2 lb) sugar; Mariposa plums 800 g (1 lb 12 oz) sugar; raspberries 850 g (1 lb 14 oz) sugar; 2 lemons per kg of fruit for raspberries; 1.5 lemons for the rest. One kilo (2 lb 3 oz) of fruit makes 4½ jars of jam. She also had the weight of the different saucepans she would use.

Every year she would retrieve this important information and make jam accordingly, using the fruit from the apricot and plum trees in the backyard. Use the same proportions to scale up or down according to the amount of fruit you have.

Apricots are quite finicky in jam making; they have to be just the right ripeness. This means they should be pale, with a tinge of green, and quite firm. These usually have a good amount of natural pectin, so you will get a jam that is nicely firm. I also let the ingredients sit in the pan for a couple of hours before cooking; this draws out some of the liquid from the fruit, which helps dissolve the sugar more evenly.

Apricot jam

MARMELLATA DI ALBICOCCHE

MAKES ABOUT 10 × 370 ML (12½ FL OZ) JARS

2 kg (4 lb 6 oz) apricots, just starting to become ripe
3 large lemons
1.5 kg (3 lb 5 oz) sugar

Wash the apricots well. Cut in half, removing the stones, and drop into a large saucepan on the stovetop.

Juice the lemons, reserving the pips and pulp. Place the pips and pulp on a square of muslin (cheesecloth) and tie it up tightly with a long piece of kitchen string. Add the lemon juice and sugar to the pan. Drop in the muslin bag and secure it to the pan handle with the string. Leave to sit for a couple of hours to help draw the liquid from the fruit.

About 20 minutes before you make the jam, wash your glass jars, and their lids, in hot soapy water and rinse well. Place the upturned jars and lids in an 80°C (175°F) fan-forced oven to dry for at least 20 minutes. Turn the oven off and let them sit in there until ready to use.

Place a small plate in the freezer to test the jam set, and have several teaspoons ready.

Back to the jam. Turn the heat on low, stirring the ingredients occasionally. Once the sugar has dissolved, turn the heat to high; the fruit will rapidly start to boil. Stir frequently so the fruit doesn't catch on the base or burn – it may spatter, so take care! After about 12 minutes of rapid boiling, you should be reaching setting point.

Remove the plate from the freezer. Carefully dip a clean teaspoon into the jam and pour it onto the plate. If the jam is thick on the plate, it is ready. If it is runny, then boil the jam for a few more minutes, return the plate to the freezer and test again with a clean teaspoon. Once you are satisfied with the jam set, turn off the heat and allow to cool for 20 minutes or so.

Carefully pour the hot jam into your jars, almost to the top, then seal. If you end up with one jar that is only partially full, store it in the fridge as soon as it has cooled down, and use that jar up first.

The hot jam in the warm sealed jars will form a vacuum that will keep the jam from spoiling. Once cool, they can be stored in the pantry for several years.

My father had been the main jam-eater in the house, spreading his jam thickly on bread with ricotta for breakfast. Once he left us, the pantry was overflowing, so Mamma started generously handing jars to friends and family whenever they dropped by – a welcome and special sweet gift with a handwritten label.

Red plum jam

MARMELLATA DI SUSINE

MAKES ABOUT 10 × 370 ML (12½ FL OZ) GLASS JARS

2 kg (4 lb 6 oz) red plums, preferably firm and not overly ripe
3 large lemons
1.8 kg (4 lb) sugar

Wash the plums well. Remove the stones, cutting the plums in half, and chopping any especially large ones into smaller pieces. Place in a large saucepan on the stovetop.

Juice the lemons, reserving the pips and pulp. Place the pips and pulp on a square of muslin (cheesecloth) and tie it up tightly with a long piece of kitchen string. Add the lemon juice and sugar to the pan. Drop in the muslin bag and secure it to the pan handle with the string. Leave to sit for a couple of hours to help draw the liquid from the fruit.

About 20 minutes before you make the jam, wash your glass jars, and their lids, in hot soapy water and rinse well. Place the upturned jars and lids in an 80°C (175°F) fan-forced oven to dry for at least 20 minutes. Turn the oven off and let them sit in there until ready to use.

Place a small plate in the freezer to test the jam set, and have several teaspoons ready.

Back to the jam. Turn the heat on low, stirring the ingredients occasionally. Once the sugar has dissolved, turn the heat to high; the fruit will rapidly start to boil. Stir frequently so the fruit doesn't catch on the base or burn – it may spatter, so take care! After about 10 minutes of rapid boiling, you should be reaching setting point.

Remove the plate from the freezer. Carefully dip a clean teaspoon into the jam and pour it onto the plate. If the jam is thick on the plate, it is ready. If it is runny, then boil the jam for a few more minutes, return the plate to the freezer and test again with a clean teaspoon. Once you are satisfied with the jam set, turn off the heat and allow to cool for 20 minutes or so.

Carefully pour the hot jam into your jars, almost to the top, then seal. If you end up with one jar that is only partially full, store it in the fridge as soon as it has cooled down, and use that jar up first.

The hot jam in the warm sealed jars will form a vacuum that will keep the jam from spoiling. Once cool, they can be stored in the pantry for several years.

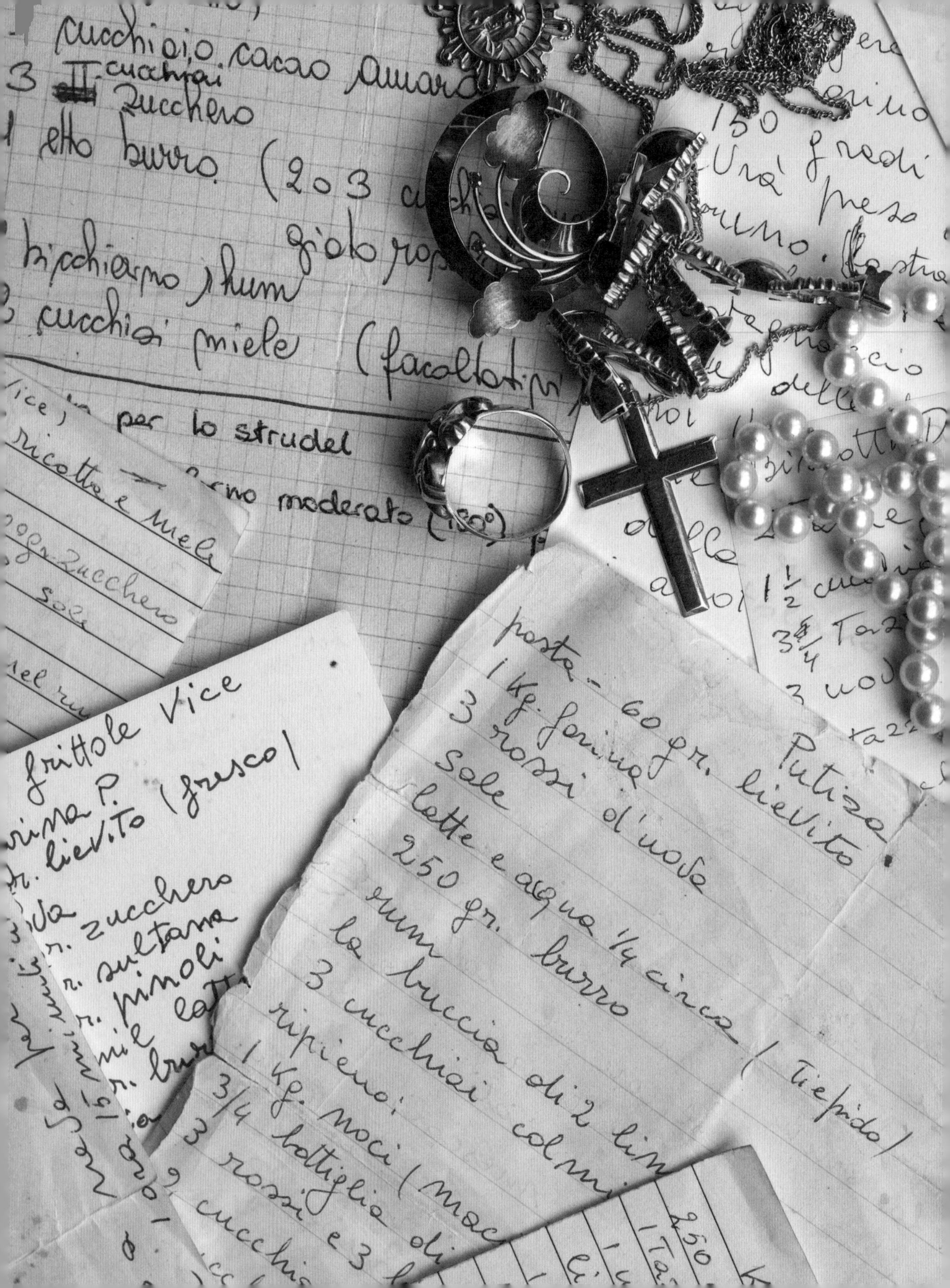

cucchiaio cacao amaro
3 II cucchiai zucchero
1 etto burro (203 cucchiai...
giallo rossi
tri chicchiarino) rum
3 cucchiai miele (facoltativi
...ice) per lo strudel
ricotta e miele forno moderato (160)
zucchero
sale
nel ru

frittole Vice
...ima P.
...r. lievito (fresco)
...va
...r. zucchero
...r. sultana
...r. pinoli
...r. miele
...r. burro

pasta.- 60 gr. lievito
1 Kg. farina
3 rossi d'uova
sale
latte e acqua 1/4 circa (tiepido)
250 gr. burro
rum
la buccia di 2 lim...
3 cucchiai colm...
ripieno:
1 Kg. noci (mac...
3/4 bottiglia di...
3 rossi e 3...
cucchiai

150 gradi
ura meso

Putiza

1 1/2 cucchiai
3 5/4 Tazi...
3 uov...
taz...

This page: Fresco in Giusti Palace, Verona (2022).
Opposite: Livia and Clara's handwritten recipes and Livia's jewellery.

Thank you

With loving thanks to my extended family for your memories of the many meals we shared with Mamma/Nonna and Papà/Nonno, and especially to my daughter, Tamara, who spent a lot of time with her nonni growing up and helping her nonna in the kitchen.

To Claire, for your story contribution on behalf of the grandchildren and your foodie support in general; to Barbara, for your help with Mamma's recipes and old photos; and to Mark, for your feedback through the whole process of testing, eating, writing and photographing the book, thank you.

Thanks also to Sam for the use of your amazing house by the beach where I spent teenage summers, and to Dean for capturing the memories of this home. To Lisa from Pidapipó, thank you for the Nonna Bacchia Gelato and to your nonna Elsie for making Mamma so happy. To Verdiana, thank you for helping me out with those forgotten recipes.

To the team at Smith Street Books: Lucy, it has been a joy to work with you again on this book and I have so appreciated your support during the health challenges I faced in 2023. To Paul, thank you for believing in this project and me; Vanessa for capturing the essence of the book in your beautiful design; Katri for editing my words; Pamela and Helena for your attention to detail.

To Emiko, Silvia and Vicky, thank you for taking the time to read my manuscript and write such beautiful words of support. I admire your work as food writers and feel privileged to know you.

And to you, dear readers, and those who follow my blog or follow me on Instagram, thank you for your connection and support of my mamma and our shared meals over the years; it has made my dream of sharing her recipes in this book a reality.

Grazie di cuore.

About the author

Paola was born in Melbourne, Australia. Her parents migrated from North-east Italy to Melbourne in 1950. Paola grew up in a family where the growing and preparation of food, the gathering of friends and shared meals were at its heart.

Paola's cooking is inspired by the home-cooked meals her mother, Livia, made, food from the Veneto, Friuli-Venezia Giulia and the northern coast of the Adriatic Sea, highlighting the fruit and vegetables that were grown in her father, Nello's, backyard garden. The dishes tell stories of her family, her origins and her love of simple and seasonal produce.

A dentist by profession, Paola realised long ago that what mattered most to her was food and cooking, and their link to her family and their homeland. She established the award-winning blog 'Italy on my mind', where she continues to share recipes, stories of family and photos. Paola regularly runs cooking classes in Melbourne and has run residential cooking workshops at the Anna Tasca Lanza Cooking School in Sicily, and food and wine tours of the Adriatic coast of Puglia and of Trieste and its surrounds. She discovered a passion for photography along the way, and her Instagram account '@italyonmymind' is full of images of Italy and its food.

Paola lives in Melbourne with her husband, Mark, and travels to Europe regularly to visit her daughter, Tamara, and immerse herself in the culture and foods of her ancestors.

Paola has written, styled and photographed three cookbooks: *Italian Street Food* (2016/re-edition 2021); *Adriatico: Recipes and stories from Italy's Adriatic Coast* (2018); and *Istria: Recipes and stories from the hidden heart of Italy, Slovenia and Croatia* (2021).

At Nonna's Table is her fourth cookbook.

Index

A

almonds
Amaretti & chocolate semifreddo 195
Buttery almond crescents 157
Cinnamon amaretti 154
Old-fashioned coconut & almond slice 160
Roasted peaches with amaretti & Marsala 169
Thin almond & lemon biscotti 150

amaretti
Amaretti & chocolate semifreddo 195
Cinnamon amaretti 154
Roasted peaches with amaretti & Marsala 169
Amaretti & chocolate semifreddo 195
Amaretti con cannella 154

anchovies
anchovy mayonnaise 73
Fish fillets with onion, anchovies & capers 119
Julius Caesar salad 73
Salmon baked with salsa verde 122
salsa verde 122
anchovy mayonnaise 73
Apple & ricotta strudel 174–6
Apricot jam 198–200

apricots
Apricot jam 198–200
Crostata with jam 162
Orange cake with apricots 182
artichokes: Schnitzels with ham, cheese & artichoke 134
Asiago: Sausage & spinach frittata 43
Asparagi gratinati 18

asparagus
Asparagus gratin with walnuts 18
Grilled vegetable platter 28
Asparagus gratin with walnuts 18
aubergines *see* eggplants

B

barley *see* pearl barley

basil
basil pesto 74
Everyday vegetable soup with basil pesto 36
Little meatballs in tomato sugo 136
meatballs 136
Peperonata with eggplant & tomato 97
Potato & tomato stew 105
Potato salad with basil pesto 74
basil pesto 74

bay
Clara's slow-cooked beef stew 147
Peperonata with zucchini & red pepper 92
Pickled vegetables 24
beans: Green beans & tomatoes 78

beef
Celebration roast chicken 128–30
Clara's slow-cooked beef stew 147
Italian meatloaf with eggs 142–44

Little meatballs in tomato sugo 136
meatballs 136
Pizza-style escalopes 133
Stuffed tomatoes 106–8
see also veal

bell peppers
Grilled vegetable platter 28
Peperonata with eggplant & tomato 97
Peperonata with zucchini & red pepper 92
Pickled vegetables 24
Red pepper braise 82
berries *see* raspberries, strawberries
Biscotti di mandorle con limone 150
biscotti, Thin almond & lemon 150
Bistecche alla pizzaiola 133
blue cheese: Figs with prosciutto & blue cheese 16

braises
Braised mushrooms 90
Red pepper braise 82
Braised mushrooms 90
brandy: Celebration roast chicken 128–30
Brasato della zia Clara 147

bread
Apple & ricotta strudel 174–6
Celebration roast chicken 128–30
crumbing 134
Focaccia with milk 44
Italian meatloaf with eggs 142–44
Julius Caesar salad 73
Little meatballs in tomato sugo 136
meatballs 136
Schnitzels with ham, cheese & artichoke 134
broccolini: Pickled vegetables 24
Brussels sprouts with pancetta 89
Buttery almond crescents 157

C

cakes
Chocolate & hazelnut log 190
Hazelnut & chocolate layer cake 185–6
Isa's pear cake 178
Night & day cake 188
Orange cake with apricots 182
Calandraca (senza carne) 105
Cannelloni ripieni della mamma 56–8
Cannelloni with ricotta, spinach & oven-roasted
tomatoes 56–8

capers
Fish fillets with onion, anchovies & capers 119
Salmon baked with salsa verde 122
salsa verde 122
capsicums *see* bell peppers

carrots
Chicken egg-drop soup 34
Everyday vegetable soup with basil pesto 36
Fettuccine with veal & mushroom ragù 50

Italian meatloaf with eggs 142–44
Little meatballs in tomato sugo 136
meatballs 136
Pickled vegetables 24
cauliflower: Pickled vegetables 24
Cavolini di bruxelles trifolati 89
celery
Chicken egg-drop soup 34
Everyday vegetable soup with basil pesto 36
Fettuccine with veal & mushroom ragù 50
Celebration roast chicken 128–30
cheese
Crepes with spinach & fontina 110–12
Sausage & spinach frittata 43
see also Asiago, blue cheese, Emmental, fontina,
    mozzarella, parmesan, ricotta, scamorza bianca
chicken
Celebration roast chicken 128–30
Chicken egg-drop soup 34
Oven-roasted chicken thighs with mustard & leeks 126
Chicken egg-drop soup 34
Chifel di mandorle 157
chilli
anchovy mayonnaise 73
Green beans & tomatoes 78
Julius Caesar salad 73
Little meatballs in tomato sugo 136
meatballs 136
Potato & tomato stew 105
Red pepper braise 82
chocolate
Amaretti & chocolate semifreddo 195
Chocolate & hazelnut log 190
chocolate icing 185
Hazelnut & chocolate layer cake 185–6
Livia's Italian trifle 172
Night & day cake 188
Chocolate & hazelnut log 190
chocolate icing 185
Ciambella giorno e notte 188
cinnamon
Cinnamon amaretti 154
Isa's pear cake 178
Cinnamon amaretti 154
Clara's slow-cooked beef stew 147
coconut
Old-fashioned coconut & almond slice 160
Orange cake with apricots 182
coffee: Hazelnut & chocolate layer cake 185–6
courgettes *see* zucchini
cream, vanilla 190
Crepe al forno con spinaci e fontina 110–12
Crepes with spinach & fontina 110–12
crescents, Buttery almond 157
Crostata di marmellata 162
Crostata with jam 162
crumbing 134
cucumbers: Pickled vegetables 24

D
dill
Salmon baked with salsa verde 122
salsa verde 122
dressing: anchovy mayonnaise 73

E
eggplant
Grilled vegetable platter 28
Peperonata with eggplant & tomato 97
eggs
Amaretti & chocolate semifreddo 195
anchovy mayonnaise 73
Apple & ricotta strudel 174–6
Cannelloni with ricotta, spinach & oven-roasted
    tomatoes 56–8
Celebration roast chicken 128–30
Chicken egg-drop soup 34
chocolate icing 185
Cinnamon amaretti 154
Crepes with spinach & fontina 110–12
Crostata with jam 162
crumbing 134
Hazelnut & chocolate layer cake 185–6
Isa's pear cake 178
Italian meatloaf with eggs 142–44
Julius Caesar salad 73
Little meatballs in tomato sugo 136
Livia's Italian trifle 172
meatballs 136
Night & day cake 188
Old-fashioned coconut & almond slice 160
Orange cake with apricots 182
pasta 56–7
Sausage & spinach frittata 43
Schnitzels with ham, cheese & artichoke 134
Thin almond & lemon biscotti 150
Emmental: Schnitzels with ham, cheese &
    artichoke 134
emulsion 44
escalopes, Pizza-style 133
Everyday vegetable soup with basil pesto 36

F
Fagiolini e pomodori 78
fennel: Pickled vegetables 24
Fettuccine con sugo di vitello e funghi 50
Fettuccine with veal & mushroom ragù 50
Fichi, prosciutto e gorgonzola 16
Figs with prosciutto & blue cheese 16
Filetti al portafoglio impanati 134
Filetti di pesce con cipolla, acciughe e capperi 119
fish
Fish fillets with onion, anchovies & capers 119
see also anchovies, salmon
Fish fillets with onion, anchovies & capers 119
Focaccia morbida con il latte 44
Focaccia with milk 44

fontina
Crepes with spinach & fontina 110–12
Schnitzels with ham, cheese & artichoke 134
Fortaia con salsiccia e spinaci 43
frittata, Sausage & spinach 43
Funghi trifolati 90

G
Giardiniera 24
grappa: Apple & ricotta strudel 174–6
Green beans & tomatoes 78
Grilled vegetable platter 28

H
hazelnuts
Chocolate & hazelnut log 190
Hazelnut & chocolate layer cake 185–6

I
ice cream
Amaretti & chocolate semifreddo 195
Roasted peaches with amaretti & Marsala 169
icing, chocolate 185
Insalata di patate con pesto al basilico 74
Insalata Giulio Cesare 73
Isa's pear cake 178
Italian meatloaf with eggs 142–44

J
jam
Apricot jam 198–200
Red plum jam 202
Julius Caesar salad 73

L
Leek prosciutto bundles 23
leeks
Everyday vegetable soup with basil pesto 36
Leek prosciutto bundles 23
Oven-roasted chicken thighs with mustard & leeks 126
lemons
Apple & ricotta strudel 174–6
Apricot jam 198–200
Asparagus gratin with walnuts 18
Chicken egg-drop soup 34
Crostata with jam 162
Isa's pear cake 178
Oven-roasted chicken thighs with mustard & leeks 126
Prawn & scallop skewers 116
Red plum jam 202
Salmon baked with salsa verde 122
salsa verde 122
Thin almond & lemon biscotti 150
Twice-cooked spinach with parmesan & lemon 81
Vanilla panna cotta with strawberries 170
lettuce: Julius Caesar salad 73
Lisa Biondi 141
Little meatballs in tomato sugo 136
Livia's Italian trifle 172

M
Marmellata di albicocche 198–200
Marmellata di susine 202
Marsala
Chocolate & hazelnut log 190
Livia's Italian trifle 172
Roasted peaches with amaretti & Marsala 169
Mayonnaise, anchovy 73
Mazzetti di porri al forno 23
meatballs 136
meatloaf, Italian, with eggs 142–44
menu planning 124–5
Minestra di verdura con pesto al basilico 36
mozzarella: Cannelloni with ricotta, spinach & oven-roasted
   tomatoes 56–8
mushrooms
Braised mushrooms 90
Fettuccine with veal & mushroom ragù 50
mustard
Oven-roasted chicken thighs with mustard & leeks 126
Salmon baked with salsa verde 122
salsa verde 122

N
Night & day cake 188
nutmeg
Celebration roast chicken 128–30
Crepes with spinach & fontina 110–12
Stuffed tomatoes 106–8
nuts *see* almonds, hazelnuts, pine nuts, pistachios, walnuts

O
Old-fashioned coconut & almond slice 160
olives
Italian meatloaf with eggs 142–44
Little meatballs in tomato sugo 136
meatballs 136
Spaghetti with oven-roasted tomato pesto 48
Stuffed tomatoes 106–8
tomato pesto 48
onions
Cannelloni with ricotta, spinach & oven-roasted
   tomatoes 56–8
Chicken egg-drop soup 34
Clara's slow-cooked beef stew 147
Everyday vegetable soup with basil pesto 36
Fettuccine with veal & mushroom ragù 50
Fish fillets with onion, anchovies & capers 119
Green beans & tomatoes 78
Italian meatloaf with eggs 142–44
Little meatballs in tomato sugo 136
meatballs 136
Parmesan risotto 62
Peperonata with eggplant & tomato 97
Peperonata with zucchini & red pepper 92
Red pepper braise 82
Rice, peas & prosciutto 61
Risotto with sausage & tomatoes 65
Stuffed tomatoes 106–8

tomato sugo 57
Zucchini & potato soup with sage 30
Zucchini with prosciutto 84
Orange cake with apricots 182

oranges
Orange cake with apricots 182
Prawn & scallop skewers 116
Vanilla panna cotta with strawberries 170

oregano
Cannelloni with ricotta, spinach & oven-roasted
tomatoes 56–8
Oven-roasted tomatoes preserved in olive oil
68–70
Pizza-style escalopes 133
Potato & tomato stew 105
Spaghetti with oven-roasted tomato pesto 48
tomato sugo 57
Oven-roasted chicken thighs with mustard & leeks 126
Oven-roasted tomatoes preserved in olive oil 68–70

P

pancetta
Brussels sprouts with pancetta 89
Fettuccine with veal & mushroom ragù 50
Italian meatloaf with eggs 142–44
Julius Caesar salad 73
Panna cotta con le fragole 170
panna cotta, Vanilla, with strawberries 170
Paparot 33
paprika: Stuffed tomatoes 106–8

parmesan
Asparagus gratin with walnuts 18
basil pesto 74
Cannelloni with ricotta, spinach & oven-roasted
tomatoes 56–8
Celebration roast chicken 128–30
Chicken egg-drop soup 34
Crepes with spinach & fontina 110–12
Everyday vegetable soup with basil pesto 36
Fettuccine with veal & mushroom ragù 50
Italian meatloaf with eggs 142–44
Julius Caesar salad 73
Leek prosciutto bundles 23
Little meatballs in tomato sugo 136
meatballs 136
Parmesan risotto 62
Peperonata with zucchini & red pepper 92
Potato salad with basil pesto 74
Rice, peas & prosciutto 61
Risotto with sausage & tomatoes 65
Sausage & spinach frittata 43
Spaghetti with oven-roasted tomato pesto 48
Spinach & polenta soup 33
Stuffed tomatoes 106–8
tomato pesto 48
Twice-cooked spinach with parmesan &
lemon 81
Zucchini with prosciutto 84
Parmesan risotto 62

parsley
Asparagus gratin with walnuts 18
Braised mushrooms 90
Brussels sprouts with pancetta 89
Celebration roast chicken 128–30
Chicken egg-drop soup 34
Everyday vegetable soup with basil pesto 36
Fish fillets with onion, anchovies & capers 119
Green beans & tomatoes 78
Grilled vegetable platter 28
Italian meatloaf with eggs 142–44
Peas & sausages 100
Prawn & scallop skewers 116
Rice, peas & prosciutto 61
Salmon baked with salsa verde 122
salsa verde 122
Sausage & spinach frittata 43
Spaghetti with oven-roasted tomato pesto 48
Stuffed tomatoes 106–8
tomato pesto 48
Zucchini with prosciutto 84

pasta
Cannelloni with ricotta, spinach & oven-roasted
tomatoes 56–8
Fettuccine with veal & mushroom ragù 50
pasta 56–7
Spaghetti with oven-roasted tomato pesto 48
pasta 56–7
Patate con le erbette 98
peaches: Roasted peaches with amaretti & Marsala 169
pearl barley: Everyday vegetable soup with basil pesto 36
pears: Isa's pear cake 178

peas
Peas & sausages 100
Rice, peas & prosciutto 61
Peas & sausages 100
Peperonata con melanzane e pomodori 97
Peperonata con zucchine e peperoni 92
Peperonata with eggplant & tomato 97
Peperonata with zucchini & red pepper 92
Peperoni rossi 82
Pesche al forno con amaretti e marsala 169

pestos
basil pesto 74
tomato pesto 48
Pickled vegetables 24

pine nuts
Apple & ricotta strudel 174–6
basil pesto 74
Everyday vegetable soup with basil pesto 36
Potato salad with basil pesto 74
Salmon baked with salsa verde 122
salsa verde 122
Spaghetti with oven-roasted tomato pesto 48
tomato pesto 48
Piselli e salsiccia 100
pistachios: Celebration roast chicken 128–30
Pizza-style escalopes 133
platter, Grilled vegetable 28

plums
    Crostata with jam 162
    Red plum jam 202
polenta: Spinach & polenta soup 33
Pollo con senape e porri 126
Pollo ripieno arrosto 128–30
Polpettine con sugo 136
Polpettone 142–4
Pomodori ripieni 106–8
Pomodori secchi 68–70
pork
    Celebration roast chicken 128–30
    Little meatballs in tomato sugo 136
    meatballs 136
    Peas & sausages 100
    Risotto with sausage & tomatoes 65
    Sausage & spinach frittata 43
    Schnitzels with ham, cheese & artichoke 134
    see also pancetta, prosciutto
Potato & tomato stew 105
Potato salad with basil pesto 74
potatoes
    Everyday vegetable soup with basil pesto 36
    Potato & tomato stew 105
    Potato salad with basil pesto 74
    Potatoes & silverbeet 98
    Stuffed tomatoes 106–8
    Zucchini & potato soup with sage 30
Potatoes & silverbeet 98
Prawn & scallop skewers 116
prosciutto
    Figs with prosciutto & blue cheese 16
    Leek prosciutto bundles 23
    Rice, peas & prosciutto 61
    Zucchini with prosciutto 84

R
raspberries: Amaretti & chocolate semifreddo 195
Red pepper braise 82
Red plum jam 202
rice
    Parmesan risotto 62
    Rice, peas & prosciutto 61
    Risotto with sausage & tomatoes 65
    Stuffed tomatoes 106–8
Rice, peas & prosciutto 61
ricotta
    Apple & ricotta strudel 174–6
    Cannelloni with ricotta, spinach & oven-roasted
        tomatoes 56–8
Risi e bisi con prosciutto 61
risotto
    Parmesan risotto 62
    Risotto with sausage & tomatoes 65
Risotto al parmigiano 62
Risotto al pomodori secchi sott'olio 65
Risotto with sausage & tomatoes 65
Roasted peaches with amaretti & Marsala 169

rum
    Apple & ricotta strudel 174–6
    Hazelnut & chocolate layer cake 185–6

S
sage
    Clara's slow-cooked beef stew 147
    Fettuccine with veal & mushroom ragù 50
    Zucchini & potato soup with sage 30
salads
    Julius Caesar salad 73
    Potato salad with basil pesto 74
Salmon baked with salsa verde 122
Salmone con salsa verde 122
salsa verde 122
sauces
    salsa verde 122
    tomato sugo 57
    see also pesto
Sausage & spinach frittata 43
savoiardi: Livia's Italian trifle 172
scallops: Prawn & scallop skewers 116
scamorza bianca: Cannelloni with ricotta, spinach &
    oven-roasted tomatoes 56–8
Schnitzels with ham, cheese & artichoke 134
semifreddo, Amaretti & chocolate 195
Semifreddo della zia Clara 195
silverbeet
    Crepes with spinach & fontina 110–12
    Potatoes & silverbeet 98
skewers, Prawn & scallop 116
slice, Old-fashioned coconut & almond 160
'Slice' di cocco e mandorle 160
soups
    Chicken egg-drop soup 34
    Everyday vegetable soup with basil pesto 36
    Spinach & polenta soup 33
    Zucchini & potato soup with sage 30
Spaghetti al pesto rosso 48
Spaghetti with oven-roasted tomato pesto 48
Spiedini di gamberi e capesante 116
spinach
    Cannelloni with ricotta, spinach & oven-roasted
        tomatoes 56–8
    Crepes with spinach & fontina 110–12
    Italian meatloaf with eggs 142–44
    Sausage & spinach frittata 43
    Spinach & polenta soup 33
    Twice-cooked spinach with parmesan & lemon 81
Spinach & polenta soup 33
Spinaci ripassati con parmigiano e limone 81
stews
    Clara's slow-cooked beef stew 147
    Potato & tomato stew 105
Stracciatella 34
strawberries: Vanilla panna cotta with strawberries 170
Strudel di ricotta e mele di Clara 174–6
strudel, Apple & ricotta 174–6

Stuffed tomatoes 106–8
sultanas: Apple & ricotta strudel 174–6
Swiss chard *see* silverbeet

T
tart: Crostata with jam 162
Thin almond & lemon biscotti 150
thyme
    Braised mushrooms 90
    Oven-roasted chicken thighs with mustard & leeks 126
tomato pesto 48
tomato sugo 57
tomatoes
    Cannelloni with ricotta, spinach & oven-roasted tomatoes 56–8
    Clara's slow-cooked beef stew 147
    Fettuccine with veal & mushroom ragù 50
    Green beans & tomatoes 78
    Little meatballs in tomato sugo 136
    Oven-roasted tomatoes preserved in olive oil 68–70
    Peperonata with eggplant & tomato 97
    Peperonata with zucchini & red pepper 92
    Pizza-style escalopes 133
    Potato & tomato stew 105
    Red pepper braise 82
    Risotto with sausage & tomatoes 65
    Spaghetti with oven-roasted tomato pesto 48
    Stuffed tomatoes 106–8
    tomato pesto 48
    tomato sugo 57
Torta arancia e cocco con albicocche 182
Torta cornelia 185–6
Torta di pere Isa 178
trifle, Livia's Italian 172
Tronco di cioccolata e nocciole 190
Twice-cooked spinach with parmesan & lemon 81

V
vanilla
    Apple & ricotta strudel 174–6
    Buttery almond crescents 157
    Chocolate & hazelnut log 190
    Cinnamon amaretti 154
    Crostata with jam 162
    Hazelnut & chocolate layer cake 185–6
    Isa's pear cake 178
    Livia's Italian trifle 172
    Night & day cake 188
    Roasted peaches with amaretti & Marsala 169
    Thin almond & lemon biscotti 150
    vanilla cream 190
    Vanilla panna cotta with strawberries 170
vanilla cream 190
Vanilla panna cotta with strawberries 170
veal
    Celebration roast chicken 128–30

    Fettuccine with veal & mushroom ragù 50
    Schnitzels with ham, cheese & artichoke 134
Verdure alla griglia 28
vermouth
    Braised mushrooms 90
    Oven-roasted chicken thighs with mustard & leeks 126

W
walnuts: Asparagus gratin with walnuts 18
wine, red
    Clara's slow-cooked beef stew 147
    see also Marsala
wine, white
    Asparagus gratin with walnuts 18
    Braised mushrooms 90
    Fettuccine with veal & mushroom ragù 50
    Fish fillets with onion, anchovies & capers 119
    Italian meatloaf with eggs 142–44
    Oven-roasted chicken thighs with mustard & leeks 126
    Parmesan risotto 62
    Peas & sausages 100
    Peperonata with zucchini & red pepper 92
    Pickled vegetables 24
    Rice, peas & prosciutto 61
    Risotto with sausage & tomatoes 65
    Zucchini with prosciutto 84

Y
yoghurt: Night & day cake 188

Z
zucchini
    Everyday vegetable soup with basil pesto 36
    Grilled vegetable platter 28
    Italian meatloaf with eggs 142–44
    Little meatballs in tomato sugo 136
    meatballs 136
    Peperonata with zucchini & red pepper 92
    Pickled vegetables 24
    Zucchini & potato soup with sage 30
    Zucchini with prosciutto 84
Zucchini & potato soup with sage 30
Zucchini con prosciutto 84
Zucchini with prosciutto 84
Zuppa di zucchine e patate con salvia 30
Zuppa Inglese 172

Published in 2024 by Smith Street Books
Naarm (Melbourne) | Australia
smithstreetbooks.com

ISBN: 978-1-9227-5474-5

Smith Street Books respectfully acknowledges the Wurundjeri People of the Kulin
Nation, who are the Traditional Owners of the land on which we work, and we pay
our respects to their Elders past and present.

Publisher: Paul McNally
Managing editor: Lucy Heaver
Editor: Katri Hilden
Designer: Vanessa Masci
Photographers: Paola Bacchia and Dean Schmideg;
     p. 201, taken by Kristoffer Paulsen
Food stylist: Paola Bacchia
Food preparation: Paola Bacchia
Proofreader: Pamela Dunne
Indexer: Helena Holmgren
Prepress: Megan Ellis

Printed & bound in China by C&C Offset Printing Co., Ltd.

Book 310
10 9 8 7 6 5 4 3 2